USBORNE TRUE STORIES

THE BLITZ

D1365016

This edition published in 2007 by Usborne Publishing Ltd,
Usborne House, 83-85 Saffron Hill, London
EC1N 8RT, England.
www.usborne.com

A catalogue record for this title is available
from the British Library

Printed in Great Britain

Edited by Jane Chisholm
Designed by Brian Voakes
Series designer: Mary Cartwright
Cover design by Michael Hill

USBORNE TRUE STORIES

THE BLITZ

HENRY BROOK

Illustrated by Ian McNee

Consultant: Terry Charman
Historian, Imperial War Museum

Contents

world had ever seen. Could the city of
Coventry survive a deadly firestorm?

STORM WARNINGS

*A Stuka dive bomber
dropping bombs*

On September 1, 1939, the German army invaded Poland. Without any warning, they smashed their way across the frontier, using dazzling new tactics that relied on speed, daring and explosive force. This became known as *Blitzkrieg*, or lightning war, a phrase coined by an American journalist describing the German attack.

Blitzkrieg was a response to the static, close-quarter trench fighting of the First World War (1914-18). In that conflict, attacks involving tens of thousands of foot soldiers, known as infantry, sometimes failed to breech the enemy lines. Barbed wire barricades and machine guns could stop the infantry in their tracks. Instead of sending ranks of soldiers across a wide battlefront, Blitzkrieg called for an attacking force to use surprise and concentrated firepower to overwhelm their opponents. Supported by dive-bomber attack planes, paratroopers and heavy artillery shelling, elite

German soldiers punched a narrow hole in the Polish frontier. Before the Poles could react, a motorized column of panzer tanks and infantry burst through – outflanking, encircling, and then crushing any resistance.

The Polish army was made up of three million men, but only about half of these were mobilized and ready for action. Their tactics and equipment were pitifully outdated and some of their best soldiers were in cavalry regiments, with a fighting tradition that stretched back to the 1400s. They carried powerful rifles and even machine guns on their horses, but were no match for the Germans' steel-plated panzers. The fighting was over in 28 days. Governments across the world looked on in astonishment at the power of Blitzkrieg.

Britain, France and Poland were bound together by a military and political alliance and news of the invasion brought a quick response from the British Prime Minister, Neville Chamberlain. He threatened the German leader, Adolf Hitler, with force, unless he withdrew his army at once. But Hitler ignored the warning and Chamberlain was left with no choice but to fight. Just two days later, at 11:15 on September 3, he made an announcement on the radio, confirming that the two countries were at war. Moments later, air raid sirens howled across London.

But it was a false alarm – a French civilian plane had flown off course over the capital. There was no sudden attack against Britain. Instead, Europe was locked in an agonizing, seven-month waiting game, while each side traded insults and propaganda, trying to win over a neutral America to their cause. The only major battles were fought at sea, as great warships swapped salvoes and German *U-boat* submarines stalked Britain's merchant ships in the Atlantic Ocean. British newspapers called it the 'phoney war' or 'bore war' and joked about a *'Sitzkrieg'* instead of a lightning war.

But, on April 9, 1940, the waiting ended with the roar of a thousand guns. Hitler unleashed Blitzkrieg against Denmark and Norway. By May 28, his troops had overrun Belgium, Luxembourg and Holland. Only a month later, the Germans had occupied much of France, forcing the British army and its allies into a desperate retreat. In a dramatic rescue operation, over 300,000 French and British soldiers were ferried across the English Channel from the beaches around Dunkirk.

Short of equipment, bruised and tattered, the forces opposing Hitler gathered in their besieged island fortress. The British were relying on their Royal Air Force and, in particular, on its *Spitfire* and *Hurricane* fighter pilots, to save the day. Royal Navy warships were there to guard the English Channel against invasion. But warships are vulnerable to attack from the air, so whoever won control of the skies would win the battle for Britain.

German strategists had developed Blitzkrieg by combining their ideas for a fast-moving, heavily armed and independent infantry with recent advances in

weapons and motorized transportation. They studied
the work of British military experts, including Captain
Liddell Hart, who compared motorized warfare to a
lightning strike. Hart's ideas were largely ignored by
his own commanders, but the Germans understood
their potential. They were particularly interested in the
role of the bomber plane, and how it might be used to
bring a country to its knees. Events in the First World
War had persuaded them of the bomber's awesome
destructive power.

At the opening of the First World War, air warfare
had been limited to slow-flying monoplanes making
spying patrols over enemy trenches. But the demands
of war often produce astonishing technological
breakthroughs. By 1915, the Germans were dropping
bombs into the heart of London from gas-filled
airships known as *Zeppelins*. These droning,
mammoth raiders only carried a small bomb load –
the same weight of explosive as a single First World
War bomber. But they had a catastrophic effect on
people's morale. The British had always considered
their island to be a safe haven, protected by the moat
of the English Channel, so they were shaken by their
sudden exposure to attack from the air.

By 1917, the Zeppelins had been driven off by
British fighter planes and *ack-ack* – anti-aircraft
gunfire – but they were soon replaced by huge *Gotha*
planes dropping high explosive bombs. There was
something alien and terrifying about these deadly
metal canisters screaming down through the night sky.

Thousands of people panicked and forced their way into London's Underground railway stations to seek shelter. Some even refused to come out after the raids. The local authorities worried that life in the city would become impossible unless they forced everyone to stay above ground.

Over 1,400 people died in the air attacks during the First World War, and British military chiefs speculated that, if huge squadrons of bombers could be built this time, they might demolish a capital city in weeks, if not days.

Throughout the 1930s, the Germans set about designing new planes for their air force, known as the *Luftwaffe*. In a move they would regret in the later stages of the war, Luftwaffe commanders decided against manufacturing a long range, heavy bomber. Instead, designers concentrated on building smaller, faster planes suitable for making sudden, precise attacks in support of their infantry. These planes could appear in the sky without any warning and spread terror on the ground with their machine guns and high explosive bombs.

The *Junkers 87 Stuka* dive bomber had first been tested in the Spanish Civil War (1936-39). With sirens fixed to its landing legs, the Stuka made a blood-chilling howl as it plunged in a near-vertical attack, earning it a nightmarish reputation across Europe. When the Germans invaded Poland, the Luftwaffe was in control of the skies within two days. It was this air power that brought the Germans within sight of England, at the end of a staggering run of victories across Europe.

But, if Hitler expected the British to shudder and beg for peace he was mistaken. There was a new Prime Minister in charge – Winston Churchill – and he was ready to fight. Churchill warned his people he had nothing to offer them in the struggle ahead but blood, toil, tears and sweat. Their lives were already blighted by the war. Rationing of food, fuel and other goods was creeping in, as the U-boats tightened their grip on British trade with the outside world. Every citizen, including babies, had been issued with gas-masks in case of poison gas attack. Local councils removed road signs, to confuse the enemy if they invaded, and they extinguished street lights as part of their blackout precautions against German spy planes. But these hardships were nothing to the horrors the country would soon be facing.

The bombers were coming, rushing towards their targets. Their mission was to crush the Royal Air Force – its airfields and equipment – and seize control of the skies over southern England to open the way for invasion. If that failed, they would pound British towns and cities until Churchill was forced to surrender.

German bombs and shells had demolished about one fifth of Poland's grand capital, Warsaw, in a matter of weeks. Now London, the world's largest metropolis, was standing directly in the path of a Blitzkrieg storm.

The British were expecting sustained and ferocious raids, by the mightiest air force in the world. People braced themselves for the bloodiest ordeal in their country's history - and they named it the Blitz.

A HURRICANE SNAPS
A PENCIL

The badge given to members of the 'Caterpillar Club'

Sergeant Ray T. Holmes was relaxing in a steaming hot bath when the siren sounded. It was the signal for every man on the airfield to get ready for action. The next instant he was pulling on the first clothes to hand as he rushed to the door. Holmes was a British fighter pilot, stationed at Hendon aerodrome. He knew that if his squadron had to 'scramble' – pilot slang for getting their planes off the ground – every moment wasted would be regretted later, up in the skies.

After months of aerial combat with the Luftwaffe, the pilots of the Royal Air Force (RAF) had learned a lot about survival. They knew how important it was to get into position and gain height on the raiders, and this all took precious minutes of flying time. Holmes was still dripping from his bath as he hauled himself into the back of a truck, joining a clutch of other pilots on the high-speed race across the airstrip towards their Hurricane fighter planes. The other men chuckled at his appearance. He was wearing a casual sports shirt instead of his RAF tunic or flight overalls. But Holmes smiled and shrugged his shoulders. It was no big deal. The pilots were flying so many combat missions they had little time for rules and regulations. Some pilots wore thick layers of clothes to fend off the cold at high altitude. And who was going to complain about their dress, as they criss-crossed the skies at 10,000 feet, fighting to save their country from invasion?

By the time the pilots reached the dispersal area where planes were parked, the airfield loudspeakers were calling SCRAMBLE. Sprinting over to a hut, Holmes yanked his locker open, pulled on some flying boots and his 'Mae West' lifejacket, then ran out into the sunshine. A team of technicians and mechanics surrounded his plane, making their final checks and preparations for take-off. Holmes climbed up to the cockpit and strapped himself in, fixed his helmet, oxygen supply and radio cable in place, then opened the throttle. His Hurricane's Rolls-Royce Merlin engine roared into life. Moments later, the plane was streaking into the air.

Holmes had four minutes to prepare himself for battle as he climbed with 11 other fighters to intercept the German raiders. A coastal radar station had detected the formation of 36 Dornier bombers - known as 'flying pencils' because of their long, thin fuselage. They were loaded with high explosives and heading straight for central London.

It was September 15, 1940, and for two months air war had been raging over southern England as the RAF and the Luftwaffe locked horns for control of the skies. The Battle of Britain, as it became known, had started on July 10 with Stuka raids on English ports and Channel shipping. The attacks quickly spread to airfields and other vital RAF targets. With a force of 2,600 bombers and fighters, the Luftwaffe outnumbered the RAF's 640 fighters by four to one. German officers naturally expected a rapid victory, using their Blitzkrieg tactics of surprise and overwhelming firepower. But the RAF had some unexpected advantages.

British scientists were pioneers in the development of radar, and the RAF had built a string of 51 bases along the south coast to give them advance warning of enemy planes crossing the Channel. This new technology was reinforced by more traditional methods: thousands of Observer Corps spotters, mostly volunteers, had been recruited to scan the skies, armed with binoculars and flasks of tea. They were efficient watchmen, usually giving the RAF at least a few minutes warning before every raid, which let them make the best use of their squadrons.

With the RAF pilots waiting for them, German bombers had to be escorted by fighter planes – *Messerschmitt 109*s – for protection. In Poland, where these fighter aircraft were never far from their airfield fuel supplies, nothing could match their technical performance. But, over England, their tanks ran dry after 20 minutes of flying, and they were up against worthy opponents: the *Hawker Hurricane* and the *Supermarine Spitfire*.

The Battle of Britain was a brutal and ruthless business. Over 500 RAF and Allied pilots died in the fighting, out of around 3,000 who took part. Survival depended on the speed of the planes and the split second reactions of the pilots at their controls. The most dangerous tactic used by the formidable Messerschmitt 109 was a high-speed dive, using the glare of the sun to hide from its prey. A 109 appeared in a flash just behind the tail of an unsuspecting RAF flyer. Its nose cannons and machine guns flamed, then a second later it was rolling away, leaving a cloud of broken, burning debris in its slipstream.

The Spitfire, with a top speed of around 580kmh (360mph) could match the performance of a 109, but Holmes' Hurricane would be outpaced and outflown by a German fighter. That didn't mean the Hurricane was a sitting duck. It was still a fast plane – at 540kmh (335 mph) – and well armed. It carried eight *Browning* machine guns hidden in its wings. Sturdy and reliable, Hurricanes could take more of a beating than the other fighters in service, making it popular with the pilots who flew in them.

Leaving the agile Spitfires to tackle any 109 escorts, the Hurricanes concentrated on attacking the slower German bombers. It was an effective tactic. On September 7, after suffering terrible losses, the

Luftwaffe turned their squadrons away from RAF targets. Instead they launched a massive bombing raid against London. This was the beginning of the Blitz.

In the early stages of the Battle of Britain, RAF fighter pilots had led a strange double life. During the daylight hours, they risked their lives in a series of vicious dogfights, which tested them to the limits. But, when the sun went down, they could stroll along to a friendly village pub and swap jokes with the locals. Did they find bridging these two worlds reassuring or unsettling? They witnessed bloodshed in the sky that must have troubled them but, in interviews, pilots say they rarely discussed their combat experiences. They were too busy trying to enjoy any time off duty.

But, when the Blitz started, the two worlds collided, as civilians were finally exposed to the full horrors of war.

On the night before his mission to stop the Dorniers, Holmes had taken the London Underground rail service into the city's West End and seen crowds of people sleeping on the station platforms. They were hiding from the German bombs, their faces haunted and strained. Only a week earlier, London's East End had erupted in flames as 300 German bombers attacked the capital. There had been raids every day since then. Even the King and Queen had nearly been hit. On September 13, six bombs landed on Buckingham Palace. The royal family was uninjured, but the raid had shocked many Londoners. How could they be protected, they wondered, if the palace itself was left open to the raiders? Holmes knew that everyone in the capital was relying on RAF fighter pilots to stop the bombers from getting through.

Holmes turned his head to glance through his Hurricane's toughened glass canopy. He repeated this movement every few seconds, searching the sky for enemy fighters. The popular image of 1940s RAF pilots sporting dandy silk scarves is grounded in truth. Some airmen actually did wear them so their necks wouldn't become chaffed with their constant twitching and craning. It was vital to keep watching behind and above. If you didn't, you could find yourself joining the exclusive Caterpillar Club. The club's name was a reference to the silkworm, which looks rather like a caterpillar. Parachutes were made from silk and if an airman used one to save his life he automatically joined the club. Bailing out of a burning plane was a nightmarish experience, but there were worse outcomes for unobservant pilots.

Holmes suddenly noticed some specks in the sky above him and at first, he thought it was a great flock of dark birds, flying ahead and to the right of his plane. He squinted until he saw the slender lines of the fuselage, the black crosses on each wing: it was the Dornier raiders, spread out across a perfect blue sky.

Staring at the formation of enemy bombers, Holmes was glad he wasn't flying solo. The Dorniers were slow and unwieldy compared to his fighter, but they packed a mean punch. Each plane had a crew of five, and they controlled up to seven machine guns. The best way to tackle them was to get in quick, fire a two-second burst and then roll away quickly without presenting the Hurricane's vulnerable belly as a target. This was one of the tricks a good squadron leader would share with his pilots. Holmes' commanding officer, John Sample, an experienced fighter ace, was one of the best.

Sample had been a member of the Caterpillar Club ever since parachuting out of a burning Hurricane over France. His bravery in the air battles above Dunkirk had earned him a DFC – Distinguished Flying Cross – and he was a determined and aggressive leader.

"Tally-ho," he called to the other pilots through his radio link. "Climb and attack."

The 12 RAF fighters were arranged in a formation of six pairs, in two parallel lines. Holmes was at the rear. He watched Sample let the Dorniers fly past, then climb steeply behind them. His pack of fighters followed, wheeled in the sky and dived, streaking towards the Germans from the right flank. Every man picked a target, hoping for an easy kill as they fumbled for the firing button mounted on the joystick.

Air combat was both terrifying and thrilling. With the Merlin engine throbbing and hammering in your ears, you picked up speed in the dive. Adrenaline coursed through your blood, making your hands shake and your mind race. But you had to concentrate on pushing the safety catch next to the firing button, to arm your machine guns. It was amazing how many pilots forgot to do this first, and found themselves desperately pressing the firing button, with an enemy plane dancing in their sights.

If your guns were primed, the instant you pressed the button, eight machine guns would flame into life. There was an ear-splitting boom, as bullets tore away the protective canvas flaps that prevented the gun barrels icing up at high altitude. The recoil from the guns was powerful enough to shake and slow your plane, as though you were being punched backwards in the sky. After two or three seconds of firing you had to break away, dive and run, already looking for the next target. The encounter in the skies passed in a flash, but in that short time your guns pumped out 500 rounds – enough to knock an enemy plane clean out of the sky.

Holmes picked his target, waited until he was no more than a few hundred yards away, then fired off a burst. The closer an RAF pilot got to the enemy, the more damage he could do. Suddenly, the air around Holmes' plane was alive with flaring tracer bullets and bursts of flame as the Dornier fought back. Holmes rolled away and dived, trying to shake off any machine gunners who might be tracking him. Satisfied he was clear of any danger, he turned sharply, ready to regroup with the other Hurricanes. But he was alone in an empty sky.

This wasn't uncommon in air combat. In all the speed and confusion of an attack, a pilot could suddenly find himself miles away from the action. Holmes knew he would soon spot his fellow pilots, swarming around the raiders. But, as he peered through the canopy, he saw something else that made him gasp: three Dorniers had slipped out of the ambush and were still on course for central London. There was no time to wait for help. Holmes rolled his plane towards the raiders and set off in pursuit.

The Germans were flying in a tight 'V' formation, and Holmes knew that to approach from behind would be suicidal. Three sets of rear machine guns would open up on him before his Hurricane was close enough to do any damage. Instead, he came up on the left side of the trio, using the nearest bomber to provide cover from the other Dorniers' guns.

Holmes hit the firing button and the next instant he was flying through thick, black smoke that blocked out the sky. He expected it to clear in seconds, but then realized it wasn't smoke at all. The bulletproof glass at the front of his cockpit was covered in jet-black goo – engine oil from the Dornier, he guessed. He watched it trickle and slide from the glass as the force of the air gradually cleared it. But still the light didn't penetrate his cockpit. There was a dark shadow hanging over his plane. It was the bomber, bearing down on him, as its shattered engine forced the

German crew to slow down directly in his path.

Holmes yanked his joystick forwards, hoping to slip under the belly of the Dornier. He was close enough to see the motionless propellers in the engine above him, with only inches to spare, as he shot under the plane's fuselage and into open sky.

When he turned back to inspect his work, Holmes saw the Dornier falling to earth, trailing smoke and oil. But the other two bombers were still nearing central London. His attack hadn't persuaded them to head for home. Holmes wondered if they were on a special mission, with some vital target to destroy. His mind wandered back to the raid on Buckingham Palace. On their present course, the Dorniers would be flying directly over it.

Holmes banked his fighter around to the right of the bombers, ready to repeat his earlier tactics. He fired his guns and watched smoke and flames curling around the outside Dornier's wing. Getting closer, he realized other British fighters had already mauled the aircraft. Its fuselage was dotted and torn with bullet holes. A flicker of white caught his eye. It was one of the German crew, trying to open his parachute inside the body of the plane. As Holmes flashed over the roof of the Dornier, he saw the man tumble out through an escape hatch. He felt a thud and the Hurricane's wing-tip shook violently. Holmes turned his head and saw parachute silk billowing around his plane. He was towing the German through the air.

Until this moment, he hadn't paused to think about the men who were crewing the bombers. He had to destroy the enemy: this was his only concern. But he was suddenly aware of the frailty of the man hanging from his wing tip. The German was no longer a vicious opponent – just a frightened and desperate human being. Holmes wanted to help him.

He dipped the wings several times, trying to shake the parachute free, but it had no effect. Then he banked sharply, until the Hurricane's wing pointed to earth. When Holmes looked again, the man was gone. If his parachute was intact, he had a good chance of survival.

But this act of compassion had cost him vital seconds: the last bomber was still set on its course, pushing relentlessly towards Buckingham Palace. There were no other British fighters in sight. Holmes gunned the engine and turned to give chase.

He noticed immediately that his Hurricane felt sluggish and unresponsive to the controls. Black, greasy liquid was seeping across the windshield. This wasn't oil from the ailing bomber's engine. His plane had obviously been hit in the last attack dive, and the engine was damaged. He still had enough power to catch the Dornier, but his slower speed and struggling engine made him wary of tackling the rear gunners. So, instead, Holmes decided on a riskier tactic. He would circle around the German plane and attack from the front – cockpit to cockpit – a blind spot for the machine gunners. With the Dornier hurtling straight at him, he would only have seconds to fire his guns and veer away. But it was his best chance of getting in close enough for a kill.

Holmes pulled ahead, banked and saw the bomber rushing towards him, only a mile off. With a combined speed of over 800kmh (500mph), the two planes were rapidly closing in on each other. Already, Holmes could see the white oval shape of the German pilot's face. The details of his features grew clearer with every heartbeat. He pressed the firing button, expecting to see the bomber's cockpit explode into fragments of glass and fire, just before he climbed away to safety. But nothing happened: his guns were empty.

The Hurricane carried enough ammunition in its wings for 20 seconds of firing and Holmes' time was up. He knew he should give up the chase, return to base and re-arm. But if he broke away, the Luftwaffe bomber would finish its mission and escape. Holmes wasn't ready to let it go.

He tugged at his joystick and flashed over the Dornier's cockpit, just as he'd been planning to do if the gun attack had proved successful. The long fuselage of the aircraft stretched before him, tapering into a thin tube that ended at the tail fins. This delicate stem at the rear of the plane gave it its nickname: the flying pencil. The bomber looked flimsy to Holmes, compared to the solid bulk of his Hurricane. He flicked his joystick again, and sliced through the Dornier fuselage with the tip of his right wing. There was a crack, as he cut the bomber in two. Then he was diving steeply away.

The men in the Dornier saw the sky open up behind them as the fuselage ripped open. With no tail section to hold it steady, the plane twisted in the air with enough force to tear its wings off. The Germans were left inside a punctured tube, tumbling helplessly out of the sky.

Planes aren't designed to survive midair collisions, but Holmes thought he'd managed it. He checked his height meter and saw he was 5km (three miles) above the ground, then adjusted the joystick to level off his dive. The plane didn't respond. He glanced at the wing, but couldn't see any damage. Then he tried again to level off.

But the Hurricane was locked on its downward course and no amount of straining at the joystick would make any difference. Holmes cut the engine's power to the propeller, in an effort to slow his plane and give himself a moment to think. But he was already racing towards the ground at maximum speed. When he glanced at the height meter again, he saw that he'd lost half his altitude. With a shudder, he realized what he had to do. It was time to join the Caterpillar Club.

Once he was out of the plane, the brightness and cold of the sky made him gasp. It had never struck him before that jumping from a plane would be difficult.

But the force of rushing air made it hard to move, and his exit from the plane was anything but graceful. He tumbled out backwards, catching a blow on his shoulder from the Hurricane's tail fin.

He blinked and realized he was falling only a few thousand feet above the tangled railway lines of Victoria Station, in the heart of London. All he had to do now was pull the G-ring on his suit and the parachute would open out above him. But his right arm was locked tight, numb from the impact with his own plane. He reached over with his other arm and tried to lift his right hand into position. Howling in pain, he forced the hand up, gripped the cold metal of the ring and pulled for all he was worth.

The next moment he was spinning under his parachute, watching his plane and the fragments of the German bomber in their death dives below him. It was only then that he saw his feet were bare. The slipstream had torn his boots and socks off, and his toes were blue with cold.

Holmes had survived scything through the bomber in his Hurricane, but he wasn't out of danger yet. He had to pull hard on the guiding ropes that controlled his parachute to avoid landing on the electrified tracks around the railway station. Slamming into a row of terraced houses just beyond the station buildings, he was dragged across a roof and slid down the back wall of a house. His parachute finally caught in some guttering and the daring RAF pilot was left hanging over a dustbin.

Holmes spotted two young women sitting outside, enjoying a Sunday afternoon tea party. He wriggled out of his harness, vaulted a fence and kissed both of them on the lips.

"I hope you don't mind," he gasped in apology. "I got a little excited."

Holmes didn't know it, but the girls weren't surprised to see him. Like thousands of other Londoners, they'd been staring up at the sky, spectators of his deadly showdown with the Dornier. There was quite a crowd outside Victoria Station, where the battered bomber had finally crashed.

A group of excited well-wishers took the barefoot Holmes to a nearby pub and treated him to a glass of brandy. After a few sips, Holmes suddenly remembered his lost fighter plane.

"It's buried," a man replied to his questions. He led the pilot out to a deep crater in the road. The momentum of the Hurricane's heavy engine, moving at high speed, had driven the plane deep into the earth. Holmes hopped down to collect a fragment of the fuselage as a keepsake, then returned to the pub. By this time, an army officer had arrived. He escorted Holmes to Chelsea Barracks for a quick medical check and more celebratory drinks.

"Now really, Sergeant," snapped the Company Commander, when he was introduced to the barefoot pilot in his civilian clothes, "do you always dress like this when you fly a Hurricane?"

They may have been reckless at times but, thanks to the bravery of pilots like Ray Holmes, the Luftwaffe's losses were so high that they soon abandoned their daylight bombing raids. By late October 1940, all their efforts had been switched to the nightly Blitz against towns and cities. The RAF had won the Battle of Britain and crushed Hitler's plans for an invasion.

Holmes flew Hurricanes for the rest of the war and then had a successful career as a journalist. In 2004, a team of archaeologists finally unearthed his old Hurricane. It had been discovered under sixty years of sand, rock, and rubbish. Holmes was invited to attend a grand ceremony, when the remains were brought to the surface.

The joystick he'd last seen in September 1940 was still intact and its gun button was set to FIRE.

Holmes' plane slicing
through the Dornier

THE BOMB WARDENS

An ARP warden's helmet

It was September 7, 1940, and Barbara Nixon was about to order her after-dinner coffee at a restaurant in London's Soho when the sirens began to wail. She was annoyed at the inconvenience of yet another air raid alert. The sirens had already sounded several times that day, echoing through the city streets, parks and squares and along the winding River Thames. Every Londoner understood the blood-chilling warning: enemy planes were approaching the capital and could arrive in minutes. Beginning with a low, rising howl, the alarm climbed to a jarring high note, hung there for a few sickening seconds, then plunged back before repeating the cycle. It was a noise that was difficult to ignore, like listening to the grating screams of a newborn baby or an animal howling in pain.

"They never come this far into town," Nixon reassured her husband. "Still, I suppose we'd better find a shelter. Where do you think we should try?"

But her husband didn't answer. He was already outside, staring up at the night sky. When she joined him in the street, Nixon gasped in horror. There was a great, mile-high streak of red flames and black smoke looming over the eastern half of London. The docks were burning. Even though the blaze was miles away, the night sky was so brightly lit Nixon could read posters and shop names along the street, and study the shocked expressions of the other spectators.

It was a nightmarish sight. German planes whirled around the massive column of smoke like angry bees, dropping high explosives into the firestorm. Some of them were making their second attack of the day, after returning from airfields in France where they had picked up more bombs and fuel.

The fire had been raging since the afternoon, when almost 1,000 enemy planes, including over 300 bombers, had raided the city. Nixon had heard the sirens, but hadn't gone out to see what was happening. She was used to the attacks on oil refineries and military targets on London's fringes. But it had never felt as though her city, her home, was being raided. This was different though. Suddenly, she felt she was really in the war.

The pavement shook and cracked beneath her feet. A stray German bomber was pounding Charing Cross Station, half a mile to the south. Nixon had never experienced the violent tremor of a bomb blast before.

"Let's go," she said firmly. "I need to get back to my post."

The battle to defend Britain – or the Home Front as it came to be known – wasn't just fought in the air.

Prime Minister Winston Churchill and his generals were relying on the bravery of millions of civilians from every walk of life to help protect their country. Nixon was a trained actress by profession. But she had found herself out of work early in 1940, when London's theatres shut their doors by order of the government. Officials believed packed buildings would lead to high death tolls in raids, so they closed cinemas, concert halls, and even dog-racing tracks.

Although some of the theatres later re-opened during the quiet months of the phoney war, acting parts were hard to find. So Nixon decided to put her spare time to good use, by helping with the war effort. She wanted to be right in the thick of things, not sitting at a telephone exchange or serving tea in a canteen. So she applied to join the ARP – Air Raid Precautions service – as an air raid warden.

Nobody seemed to know exactly what the job entailed, other than helping civilians prepare for raids, but Nixon hoped to see plenty of action. In London, wardens were assigned to a number of posts within each borough. Nixon was given a tin helmet – painted with a large, white W – some blue overalls, a gas mask and a whistle, then she was sent to a post with 11 other wardens.

After a week or two, she began to understand her duties. Wardens were responsible for the safety of the local community and for maintaining its air raid shelters. They also had to report falling bombs – known officially as 'incidents' – to telephone operators at a central control room, who would decide on the appropriate emergency response. But it was still early in the war, and so far there had been no air raids to deal with. Most of Nixon's efforts went into enforcing wartime regulations and, in particular, the much-hated blackout.

On September 1, 1939, the government had made it illegal to show any kind of light after nightfall. The idea was to make it impossible for enemy pilots to navigate using the glittering landmarks of towns and cities. Every streetlight and illuminated shop sign had to be switched off, and doorways and windows blacked out using grills, shutters, thick cloth, cardboard or tape. Bus and train windows were no exception, and passengers could only peer through small diamond cutaways in the blackout material to read the names of stations. Even car headlights had to be covered, except for a thin horizontal strip that directed the beam down onto the road. There was a sharp rise in accidental deaths when the blackout came into force, as people stumbled off busy pavements, fell into canals and rivers, or became lost in unfamiliar, gloomy streets.

Fog was another hazard. Before new laws improved Britain's air quality in the 1950s, London and other big cities suffered occasionally from choking fog clouds, known as pea-soupers because they were so thick. The pea-soupers made life even more dangerous for people struggling home in the blackout.

After months of public grumbling, the authorities relaxed some of the rules. Streetlights and traffic lights came back on, but only dimly. Walkers were permitted to carry flashlights to track their way home and wardens painted ramps and other obstacles with bands of white stripes, to make them easier to see. But the blackout was still strictly policed. One man was arrested and fined for striking a match in a dark street, even though he was only trying to light his pipe. Wardens patrolled driveways, backyards and rooftops, and anyone who forgot to cover a window or close a door could expect to be scolded with the cry: *Put that light out*. Many people resented all these restrictions and thought ARP workers were no better than snoopers. Wardens had other unpopular tasks, too. Chief among them was the struggle to make everyone carry a gas mask.

The horrors of poison gas attacks in the First World War had persuaded government ministers that every citizen should be issued with a protective, rubber gas mask. By the start of the Second World War, they had distributed around 38 million of these, with specially adapted designs for babies and children, and even horses. But they were cumbersome and heavy. So, after the first year of the war brought no gas raids, few people bothered to carry them. Gas was never used during the Blitz – perhaps because the Germans didn't want to provoke any revenge gas attacks against their own cities? But it was the wardens' job to encourage people to take the threat seriously. To promote awareness, they painted mailboxes with a special paint that changed from yellow to green when exposed to poison gas. And they had other, more drastic methods to keep the general public on their toes. Wardens sometimes arranged mock raids, releasing clouds of painful tear gas in busy streets, a tactic that didn't improve the ARP's popularity.

But any ill feeling about busybody, self-important wardens was quickly forgotten when the bombs started falling. One moment people were complaining about ARP little-Hitlers, the next they were begging for their help.

Barbara Nixon's post was in the basement of an old terraced house, equipped with all the essentials: a dartboard, a dented kettle and a telephone. The room hadn't been reinforced or bomb-proofed in any way, and if a raid got particularly sticky, the wardens had been advised to take cover in a concrete pillbox located across the street. But this hidey-hole was only for the direst emergencies. Wardens weren't supposed to hide from danger during raids. Instead, they roamed the streets, reporting bomb damage and keeping an eye out for anyone trapped, injured or dead.

Nixon had wanted to play a part in the war effort – and she was about to do so. Reaching her post on the night of September 7, she met a senior warden who asked her to join him on a tour of the public shelters. They set off at once, hurrying through dark streets lit only by the lightning flashes of nearby explosions.

London had already suffered several raids before this one, even though Hitler had forbidden any bombing of civilian areas across the United Kingdom. The first explosions came on the night of August 24, when three German planes attacking an oil depot to the east dropped their bombs over the inner city by mistake. Churchill immediately ordered the RAF to retaliate, by sending 81 bombers to Berlin. The damage they caused was only slight, but Hitler was infuriated by Churchill's bravado. The man he'd promoted to run the Luftwaffe, Hermann Goering, had promised his master that no enemy plane would ever cross into German airspace. Ten days later, on September 4, an enraged Hitler lifted his ban protecting civilian targets. Now he threatened to raze – or demolish – Britain's towns and cities. The Luftwaffe wasted no time in assembling a huge attack force of bombers to carry out his wishes.

The August raid and dozens of false alarms had accustomed Londoners to the chore of traipsing out to the shelters for a few miserable hours of discomfort, while they listened to the faraway booming of exploding bombs. But nothing had prepared them for 'Black Saturday' – September 7, 1940. The Luftwaffe pounded London continuously for ten long hours, sending tons of explosives crashing into the residential areas of the city, far from any military targets. Nixon visited nine public shelters that evening. Most were surface shelters, long brick and concrete huts fitted with wooden benches, paraffin lights and a bucket for a bathroom. Around 50 people huddled inside each one, restless and scared in the gloom. Thinking the attack would be over in minutes, they hadn't brought food, drink or blankets when they had left their homes. By ten o'clock, they started to complain that if the raid didn't end soon, they'd miss last orders at the local pubs.

Nixon felt awkward and tense when confronted by their desperation. They didn't just want protection; they craved reassurance. Trembling with nerves herself, as blasts shook the walls, Nixon tried her best to appear calm and cheerful. Wardens had to be morale-boosters, on top of everything else, and in the months to come Nixon would make good use of her skills as a stage entertainer – leading sing-alongs, telling stories and trying to get smiles from her dejected audience.

By three in the morning, the bombing had become a ferocious roar of explosions, accompanied by the oppressive drone of enemy aircraft circling overhead. A quiet pint in the pub was the last thing on anyone's mind. People were just praying to hear the all-clear signal – a single, uninterrupted note from the sirens – telling them that they'd survived the night.

Nixon was caught out in the open when the attack reached its climax, dashing between two shelters. She had to hide in a doorway from the storm of dust, flying bricks and flames. Fighting to keep her composure as the buildings shook around her, she wondered how the city could survive. And how would she cope when she was confronted with human casualties? The only blood Nixon had ever seen close-up was stage make-up. She dreaded the sight of her first corpse. Putting all this to the back of her mind, Nixon went on with her patrol until the all-clear finally sounded at dawn.

London was a changed city after the mauling it suffered on Black Saturday. Over 400 people had been killed, thousands were seriously injured and whole communities around the area of the docks had lost their homes. Fires still raged hours after the attack and a black plume of smoke hung ominously over the city. Nixon watched the weary shelterers emerging into the sunlight, rushing home for a change of clothes and some breakfast before starting their day. People were still determined to get on with 'business as usual' – one of Churchill's wartime catchphrases – but nobody was pretending life was the same.

While newspaper headlines boasted LONDON CAN TAKE IT, thousands piled into the railway stations, desperate to escape another raid. The roads were jammed as many of the wealthier families left the city, some to stay with relatives, others showing up at country hotels pleading for rooms. Money gave them the option of leaving, but most Londoners were too dependent on their jobs, homes and family ties even to think of it. They got back to business as usual in their besieged districts, because they had no other choice.

Nixon got on with her own work. The sirens were sounding six or seven times a day now. At the start of the Blitz, London suffered 57 successive days of raids so she was always busy. When there were no raiders overhead she worked alongside the people in her local ward, helping them build their own bomb shelters.

One of the most famous symbols of the Blitz was the *Anderson shelter*, named after the government minister who had ordered its design. It was a small hut made of corrugated steel sheets, designed to survive anything except a direct hit. The British – always keen gardeners – dug up their lawns and buried over two million Andersons during the war. Local councils delivered them as flat packs, to be bolted together and covered with a thick layer of earth for extra protection. The shelters were roughly 2m (six feet) square and could hold four narrow bunks. Some people tried to make them look homely, planting flowers around the entrance and hanging family portraits inside.

But, on an icy winter night, most Andersons made miserable lodgings. They were prone to flooding and didn't keep out the cold or the noise of a raid. But they offered better protection than a cellar or cupboard under the stairs. Ugly and uncomfortable, Andersons saved thousands of lives, and were so hardy they can still be found today, relics of war, lost under decades of weeds in London's suburban gardens.

The security of an Anderson was only available to people with their own lawn or backyard. So most Londoners had to find other safe places, usually in public shelters, church crypts, and the basements of large buildings or Underground stations. The city's parks were criss-crossed with trenches – usually waterlogged – dug for anyone caught in the open during a raid. Up to 15,000 people even made the journey down to Chislehurst in Kent every evening to escape the Blitz, bedding down in a network of caves.

It wasn't until March 1941 that the government began distributing a shelter that families could assemble indoors. The *Morrison shelter*, named after another Cabinet minister, was a large, waist-high steel cage that was sturdy enough to withstand the weight of a collapsing house. But people hated crawling inside these claustrophobic metal boxes, and many found it impossible to sleep in any kind of shelter, and never visited one. Even in November 1940, at the height of the Blitz, a survey of Londoners revealed that half carried on working during the raids, or refused to leave the comfort of their beds. Only five percent of the people questioned spent their nights in the city's Underground stations.

Some people stubbornly ignored the Blitz altogether. After one ferocious raid on a block of terraced houses, a fireman came across an old woman in her ruined kitchen, stirring a huge pot of soup. The kitchen had no roof and was missing a wall or two, but she kept stirring as though nothing had happened.

When the fireman tried to escort her from the tottering building she protested fiercely, even when he pointed out that her precious soup was full of bricks and lumps of plaster.

There were still plenty of Londoners who did want help though. Nixon was worked off her feet and she quickly won the trust and respect of her fellow wardens and those she helped. But she continued to suffer nagging doubts about how she would react to her first sight of blood. She knew it was only a question of time – tales of carnage and havoc were coming in from all over the city – but so far her borough had suffered only light casualties. It wasn't until the tenth day of the Blitz that Barbara Nixon finally faced her demons.

On that day, she was cycling through a run-down suburb of narrow streets, a few miles from her post. It was late afternoon and still light, but in the last few days there had been several daylight raids. Nixon had no idea if there were enemy planes over London as she cycled along. With dozens of siren alerts that morning, she couldn't remember if the last one had been a warning or the all-clear. The question was soon resolved. As she glanced up at a tall, decrepit building just ahead of her, Nixon saw it suddenly bulge and swell. At the point when she thought it must burst open, all the glass in the windows fell out and the deflated building sagged back onto its foundations. The next instant, she was caught in the shockwave from a powerful blast in the next street. The ballooning building had protected her from the initial explosion, but she was still thrown through the air, and landed heavily against some railings. Jumping to her feet, Nixon heard the engine throb of a raider overhead and realized what had happened. Then she blew her whistle, because it seemed like the only sensible thing to do.

An old woman appeared in the street, demanding to know what all the fuss was about. Nixon told her the area had just been bombed, but the woman was so deaf – perhaps from the roar of the explosion – that the stunned warden was forced to perform a frantic mime to get the message across. After pointing her in the right direction for a shelter, Nixon started walking towards the origin of the blast. She had to check for any survivors who might have been bombed-in under damaged buildings. She walked slowly, conscious that in a daylight raid, with no warning, there were bound to be casualties. As she turned the corner, she saw a pile of clothes lying in the middle of the road. It was the remains of a baby, torn apart by the explosion.

Nixon found some cloth and carefully covered the child. Glancing around, she noticed other bodies strewn in the rubble, their skin and clothes covered in a layer of fine brick dust that made them look like clay dummies. Bomb victims were often found coated in this dust, making them look as though they'd been unearthed from some ancient tomb. Nixon used blankets to wrap the bodies, arranging them as best she could. Soon, other wardens were arriving on the scene, bringing ropes and stretchers. They called in a *Heavy Rescue* squad of engineers and diggers and began searching for buried survivors. Local residents who'd been away at work were soon circling the site, calling out the names of their relatives and friends. In the terrible lottery of the Blitz, lives had been changed forever in a split second. Eleven people were dead, and many more were injured. Nixon paced around the bomb site, working quickly and efficiently to help the wounded, never stopping to think about how she was coping with the horror of the attack. Finally, she had conquered her fears.

Barbara Nixon was only one of over one and a half million people who volunteered to join the ARP. She served through the bloodiest months of the Blitz and helped to save hundreds of lives. Later in the war, she trained to be an instructor, giving lectures on the principles of dealing with bomb damage, first aid and protecting the public. When peace finally came, she went back to her profession as an actress, working in television and radio for several years before retiring to the country.

RUNNING FOR HOME

During the Blitz, thousands of children were sent away from home to the safety of the countryside.

The two boys had already spent a night and a day in the village hall, along with dozens of other children. There was nothing to do but sit and wait. Every few minutes, one of the local women would come in and wander slowly among the rows of anxious youngsters. If she liked the look of a child, she called them forward for an examination.

"No lice, I hope?" the woman snapped at a billeting officer who was supervizing the children. "Some of these city kids look as though they've never been washed."

The boys glanced at each other and shrugged. They had been picked out a few times themselves, but always failed the close inspection. Nobody wanted two scruffy brothers, when they could choose a pretty little girl with blonde curls instead. All the children were evacuees, looking for someone to offer them a home. Their parents had agreed to send them away from the city streets – pocked and scarred by German bombs – to the safety of the country. But life in a small village can be just as cruel and ugly as in any shabby, city slum. As soon as they arrived, the children had been made to sit and present themselves to their potential guardians, like cattle being exhibited at a country show.

It was getting late, and it looked as though the two brothers would have to spend another night curled up on the rough, wooden beds, using their gas mask cases as pillows. The elder boy, John Beachem, was ten years old. He fingered the name tag around his neck, a crumpled square of yellow cardboard tied on with string.

"Ken," he whispered to his eight-year-old brother. "Slip out through the back door. I'll meet you outside. We're going home."

Following the bloody conflict of the First World War, politicians and generals argued about the best way to protect people in any future war. The experts were divided on many things, but they all shared one common fear: the air raid.

In 1932, Stanley Baldwin, a government minister, voiced the pessimism of the armed forces when he warned the House of Commons: "The bomber will always get through."

Baldwin believed it was impossible to prevent huge fleets of enemy planes from attacking Britain's cities. He expected thousands of civilians to die. Using a macabre algebraic equation, which predicted how many people each ton of explosive would kill, a committee of civil servants and RAF strategists calculated that a single raid on London would result in 58,000 deaths. Some doom-mongers thought air raids would annihilate whole cities, leaving the country a scorched wasteland. So, fearing the worst, ministers began talking about evacuation - the mass-movement of civilians away from possible target areas.

In the summer of 1938, Hitler's army was threatening Czechoslovakia, and a war in Europe looked certain. Local councils in Britain's industrial and military areas began asking parents to register their children for evacuation. A few years earlier, during the Spanish Civil War, the German 'Condor Legion' had bombed civilians. This outrage proved a powerful incentive for most families to go along with the scheme. On the day Germans crashed into Poland, the British government gave the order to evacuate. Within 36 hours, over one million children and 300,000 carers and parents were moved to pre-selected reception areas in the countryside, most riding on crowded trains and buses. It was an incredible feat of planning and organization. Station platforms heaved with thousands of excited infants – some weeping, some whooping – all issued with name tags and a ration of chocolate to see them through the journey.

But the meticulous planning sometimes fell apart when the evacuees reached their reception areas. Village officials complained that they hadn't been warned about the numbers expecting to be housed, fed and schooled. They were confused about the proper rations and allowances that the government had promised to anyone taking a child into their home. And the selection process itself could turn into an embarrassing – even traumatizing – ordeal for the children. If they weren't picked out within a few hours, they could be dragged from door to door looking for shelter. Some even suffered the humiliation of having their heads shaved to rid them of lice. Head lice were a serious health problem in city areas and 20% of evacuees carried them.

But these miseries were nothing compared to the despair many of them felt. They had no idea how long the fighting would last and when they might see their families again. John and Ken Beachem knew all about homesickness. They had already been evacuated twice and they were longing for home.

The Beachem boys came from a working-class area in the city of Bristol, made up of terraced houses, cobbled streets and corner pubs. Their father had died when they were very young, and the boys were brought up by a trio of hard-working women: their mother, aunt and grandmother. Money was tight, but the Beachems knew how to enjoy themselves. Ken and John had a gang of local friends and their mother was a gifted singer who performed in bars and clubs. The first year of war had brought few changes for the family, although food rationing and price rises made their lives a bit tougher. Bristol wasn't an important target for the Germans, so lots of parents decided not to evacuate their children.

There were occasional raids, but the boys saw them as an opportunity for new adventures. They played on bomb sites, building secret dens in the ruined houses, and spent hours searching for pieces of shrapnel. These metal shards from planes, artillery shells and bombs were so treasured they were traded for comics and sweets in the schoolyard. During the Battle of Britain, the boys watched the skies for enemy planes, and cheered when they spotted a dogfight between two pilots. The war seemed distant and exciting, a magnificent and thrilling contest, blazing away over the horizon.

But, in 1942, Bristol was pounded in a series of heavy air raids. The Luftwaffe had abandoned their attempts to crush the RAF and force London into submission. Instead, they redeployed their bombers over British ports, hoping to disrupt the country's transatlantic supply routes. If ships weren't able to dock and unload their cargoes, the British war effort would be hit hard. The busy port of Bristol was one of these new targets.

Ken's first brush with the Blitz came as he was walking home from the shops. With a loaf under each arm – the family's precious bread ration – he still managed to break into a sprint when he heard the sirens. He was taking a shortcut through a bomb site of smashed houses when an explosion knocked him off his feet. Ken lost consciousness for a few seconds and when he came to his senses he found himself covered in dust, sprawled across a mound of bricks. One of his shoes had been ripped off and both the loaves had disappeared. He managed to limp home, and met his grandmother on the doorstep.

"My foot's bleeding," Ken sobbed.

His grandmother was a formidable woman. She thought nothing of doing her ironing during an air raid, and refused to go anywhere near the family's Anderson shelter.

"Never mind your bleeding foot," she snapped. "Where's our bread?"

When Ken's mother heard what had happened she contacted the evacuation officials. And so, in the summer of 1942, Ken and John joined thousands of other schoolchildren being shipped around the country. They were evacuated to the seaside.

In peacetime, Weston-Super-Mare had been a popular beach resort, only 32km (20 miles) to the west of Bristol. Ken and John wondered if their evacuation might turn out to be fun – full of lazy days swimming in the sea and lounging on the sand. But they were soon disappointed. The beach had been covered in barbed wire and gun emplacements, to guard the coast against invasion. The town itself was cold and dreary and they didn't get along with their foster family. Mrs. Sandford was a stern, middle-aged woman who ruled over the rest of her clan. Her husband was a war veteran who had lost the lower part of his right arm. He covered the stump with a sock, held in place with rubber bands.

Ken and John shared a room with three other boys from Bristol, with only a double bed for all five of them. As the smallest of the boys, Ken had to sleep across the end of the bed, with four pairs of feet jostling him through the night. The Sandfords made the evacuees eat at a separate table in a corner of the kitchen and beat them if they were disobedient. This harsh treatment continued at school, where the boys were treated as outsiders and bullied. It didn't take long for them to start plotting an escape.

There was only one snag. The boys knew that one of the reasons the Sandfords had taken them in was to get extra rations. After almost three years of war, most foods and other shop goods in the United Kingdom were strictly controlled. There was a thriving black market in fresh meat, clothes and fuel, but this was only open to people with cash to spare. Most families had no choice but to tighten their belts and survive on the food coupons in their ration books. These were exchanged for goods in the shops. Evacuees earned foster parents a small allowance from the government, but their individual ration books were far more precious.

The boys thought they would need their ration books back in Bristol, but they were hidden away in Mrs. Sandford's bedroom bureau. As the smallest, and most nimble, Ken was given the job of retrieving them.

But the Sandfords kept a gate locked on the landing of the house and the only way to reach their bedroom was by inching over a greenhouse roof. Ken made his way across, slipped through the bedroom window, and quickly pocketed the ration books before sneaking past his sleeping foster parents. It was only when he was back in the boys' bedroom that he discovered he'd swiped the Sandfords' books as well.

"Never mind that," hissed John. "Let's get going."

The five boys tiptoed down the stairs and hurried out into the street. Their plan was to hide at the railway station until the first train to Bristol arrived, then ride home as stowaways. They were just crossing the station footbridge when John saw a man in a uniform lumbering out of the dark. "It's a copper," he whispered urgently. "Everybody hide."

Trapped between the bare walls of the footbridge, the boys' only hope was to pretend to be a pile of luggage. They fell into a heap on top of one another and dragged their coats over the top. But the policeman wasn't fooled, and he promptly escorted them back to their foster home.

The Sandfords were furious, both at the escape attempt and the theft of their ration books. The boys all suffered at the end of Mr. Sandford's stump but Ken received the worst beating for his role as cat burglar. It was a grim time. Any hope of escape was gone, as the ration books were guarded more carefully than ever. But when one of the evacuees had a visit from his mother, he discovered something interesting. It turned out that anyone could simply apply for a new ration book if they moved to a new area. The boys didn't need to worry about their books after all.

Ken and John went to school the next day, but when the last class finished they simply started walking out of town. It didn't take long for them to hitch a ride. That night, they were back home, sleeping in their own beds.

With the war rumbling on, Bristol's evacuation officers were soon putting pressure on Mrs. Beachem to send her boys away again. Their next foster home was even tougher. The boys were placed with a family in a Wiltshire town, and were scrubbed with floor brushes every night at bathtime. It was a welcome relief when the house received a direct hit during a daytime air raid. Luckily the boys were safe in school when it happened. They returned home, but were soon packing their bags again. This time it was a long bus ride south to the village hall in Cheddar, Somerset, where they waited to be chosen like goods on display.

It was getting dark by the time the two boys had left the village behind them. There was a light rain falling and the only shelter they could find was a small, stone cowshed. Snuggling down into their coats, Ken and John huddled together in the shed and tried to open a can of corned beef they'd brought with them from

Bristol. But the only tools they had were some sharp stones and try as they might they couldn't puncture the can. They fell asleep in each other's arms, hungry, cold and frightened.

The morning sun revived them. Aching and hungrier than ever, they scouted around until they spotted a small farm with an enclosure for chickens. Perhaps they could scavenge some fresh eggs and get a fire going to cook them? Eggs were a luxury in the war. People in the cities had to make do with a revolting, dried egg powder that tasted nothing like the real thing. While the boys were foraging in the hen house, the farmer's wife came out and offered them some breakfast. She didn't ask any awkward questions. When John told her they were on their way home she asked her husband to give them a lift to the next village.

The boys were in good spirits as they trundled down a hill on the back of the farmer's tractor. John was even happier when the man began calling over his shoulder and pointing out local landmarks. "You can see Wales over there," he shouted, lifting an arm.

"Wales is near Bristol," John whispered to his brother. "Now we know our way back. Let's run for it before we get to the village. Someone might see us there and start asking questions."

The next instant the two boys jumped down and hid in some bushes, letting the farmer rumble away without noticing their departure.

They walked all day and into the night, catching

some sleep curled up in a sodden haystack. The next morning, they met some friendly land girls - volunteers who helped to work the land during the war - who gave them apples and fresh vegetables to eat. One of the girls offered to carry the boys a few miles on her tractor. When she turned off the road, they decided to try thumbing for more rides. They were both exhausted, and the prospect of a quick journey home seemed worth the risk of being picked up by a passing police car.

Fuel was hard to come by during the war and the roads were very quiet. The first car to arrive was driven by a man wearing the white collar of a clergyman. This symbol of authority made John a little nervous, but the man offered the boys some chocolate and was immediately accepted as an ally.

"Where are you off to?" the man asked politely, once they were moving along the road.

"Bristol," replied Ken.

"But that's in the other direction," replied the man.

"It can't be," John spluttered. "We were told this was the right way for Wales, and that's over towards Bristol."

"Wales?" chuckled the man. "You must mean the town of Wells...?"

"But I've never even heard of Wells," cried Ken, suddenly remembering that their friend the farmer had a very thick country accent. Had he really said Wells, instead of Wales?

"Wells is this way, I promise you," the man laughed. "I'm the Dean of the Cathedral there, so I should know."

While Ken and John were still gasping at the news that they had spent two days hiking in the wrong direction, the Dean turned into the driveway of a large villa. It was his own house. He showed the boys into the kitchen and left them with his housekeeper. She gave them rice pudding and jam sandwiches – jam was another luxury for children of the Blitz. When the Dean returned, he asked them if they would like to meet some other evacuees from Bristol. He led them to a house in the town, where they were in for another surprise. Two of their old schoolmates had been placed there, and the Dean arranged for Ken and John to join the family. The four friends chatted late into the night, and Ken and John heard nothing but praise for their new foster parents.

"All the same," said Ken quietly, "there's no place like home."

In the morning, the Beachems accompanied their friends to school but said farewell to them at the gates. An hour later, they were tramping through open countryside.

Ken Beachem was still irritated that he'd been so badly off track when they'd begun their march. He was certain they were only about 20km (12 miles) from home, but during the war years it was difficult to check where you were. Local councils had removed most of their road signs, thinking this would baffle any enemy invasion force. As a precaution against getting lost again, Ken had spent an hour studying an atlas that morning. He'd tried to memorize the route to Bristol and was determined not to veer from it. By keeping off the roads, he reasoned the police wouldn't spot them. He was also keen to avoid any more delays caused by well-meaning strangers crossing their path.

The boys walked for hours. For lunch, they devoured the school lunches their friends had sacrificed for them. By nightfall they were tired and hungry again. A thick fog came swirling around them, and the two brothers joined hands and sang songs to keep themselves awake. Ken was almost asleep on his feet when bright lights suddenly dazzled his eyes and an army jeep screeched to a halt.

"Need a ride, kid?" a man called. It was an American soldier, at the head of a convoy of trucks. The next thing they knew, they were being lifted into the back of one of the trucks and a dozen GIs – American infantrymen – were plying them with chewing gum and chocolate. The soldiers were returning from a night exercise, and when they reached their base they offered the boys a bed for the night. Ken and John slept late into the morning, then begged a lift on a supply truck that was heading for Bristol.

By nine in the evening, the two brothers were standing with their noses pressed against the windows of a Bristol public bar. Their mother was inside, singing her heart out for a group of assembled soldiers, sailors and airmen. The Beachem boys had made it home again.

Ken and John weren't the only children who were evacuated several times in the course of the war. It was quite common for evacuees to yo-yo between home and a series of different reception areas, and many of them struggled to get used to country life and the ways of their new foster families. By spring 1940, most of the first wave of evacuees had returned home.

There were many reasons why the initial evacuation failed. During the quiet months of the phoney war, parents began to question whether it was really necessary to keep their children in the countryside. War rations made it difficult to get fuel, and rail fares had soared, so it was too expensive for most people to visit their families. The parents who chose to accompany their children often resented the power of foster parents and local officials. They also missed their friends and the reassuring hustle and bustle of town life.

But the evacuation officials learned from their mistakes. A second evacuation began in September 1940, when the bombs really started dropping. This time, the government helped families to pay their own way in the reception areas. They offered them an allowance to rent their own homes, and made road and rail fares more affordable.

Around four million people were evacuated to

escape the Blitz. Another two million people made their own private arrangements to leave the towns and cities. It was the greatest movement of people the country had ever seen and exposed thousands of wealthy middle-class families to the suffering of the poor. Britain had terrible city slums and widespread poverty in the decades before the war and evacuation brought these issues into the limelight. Immediately after the war, in the summer of 1945, a new government reformed the whole system of state benefits, social housing and health care.

As for John and Ken Beachem, their return to Bristol was short-lived. They were to have two more foster families – both in Exeter – before the war was over. Their first house was blown to pieces by a stray bomb while the brothers trembled in its Morrison shelter. So they were moved on to another foster family, eventually escaping with coins pinched from a church collection tray to pay for their bus tickets home. Ken went back to the church two decades later, and donated to its restoration fund by way of apology.

The war was almost over when they arrived back in Bristol, but they had another long journey ahead of them. Their mother married a New Zealand serviceman, and took her boys across three oceans to live with his family. Ken and John settled, at last, in the city of Wellington, New Zealand.

DANGER UNDERGROUND

Down in the Underground stations, people thought they were safe from bombs.

Bounds Green station was busy that evening. Hundreds of people were getting ready to bed down for the night, packed together along its narrow platforms. Some in the crowd had lost their homes and had nowhere else to go, but most were just seeking shelter underground. Up on the surface, bombs were falling and sirens wailing in a German air raid. The dirt and discomfort of the station seemed a small price to pay for safety and a few hours of undisturbed sleep, away from the fury of the Blitz.

At half-past nine the trains were still running, so nobody had moved their bedding down between the tracks or into the suicide pit – the trench running under the live power rail. People were sitting on the floor chatting, playing cards, listening to radios and flicking through newspapers. It was a peaceful, friendly atmosphere down in the station, as every man, woman and child tried to put the war to the back of their mind.

But cruising 8km (five miles) above London, a German bomber pilot was studying the patchwork of fires, ack-ack explosions and silver barrage balloons scattered below him. He barked an order and his crew released a coffin-sized bomb from the belly of the plane. It took 16 seconds for the bomb to fall to the ground. In the last few seconds, it began to whistle through the air in a high-pitched screech. But the people in the Underground station heard nothing. They were huddled together on the platform, laughing and talking, when the ceiling suddenly tore open and the lights flickered and died.

At the height of the Blitz, more than 100,000 Londoners were sleeping below ground every night, using their city's Underground rail network as a vast bomb shelter. They occupied 79 stations, dozing on the platforms, curling up on the escalators and bedding down between the rails after the live-electricity cables were shut down for the night. Some parents sent their children underground as soon as school was over for the day. The children staked out good spots on the platform for the rest of their family, who would arrive soon after finishing work. Petty criminals and gangsters even marked out prime spots and sold them off to the highest bidders.

The government had always tried to deter Londoners from taking cover in the Underground. They worried that train services would be disrupted and that if people became too scared to return to the surface, the whole mechanism of city life would quickly grind to a halt. But they needn't have worried. Only a few hundred Londoners remained in the tube during the day, most because they had been bombed out of their homes and local councils hadn't managed to re-house them.

Once the authorities accepted the situation, they began to improve the facilities. Council workers installed chemical toilets and first-aid tents. They set up bunk beds along the platforms, drove off the petty criminals and organized games, sing-alongs and story-telling sessions for the packs of roaming children. Actors and musicians gave performances and there were mobile libraries where people could borrow books and newspapers. Although the tube shelters were used by a relatively small number of people, they became a powerful symbol of the war at home. The newspapers presented them as an example of a united community showing the Blitz spirit of courage and defiance. But the people who used the tube shelters weren't interested in all this morale boosting; they just wanted to escape the bombs that were raging on the surface. Seeing the awful violence of the Blitz, and how it reached into every corner and crevice of their city, they knew nobody was ever really safe – even hidden in the bowels of the earth.

Alan Seymour had been a landscape artist before he joined the London Ambulance Service at the outbreak of war. As a painter, he must have been struck by the amazing light display of the air raids, the vivid explosions set against the total darkness of the blackout. But Seymour rarely had a spare moment to gaze up at the strange beauty of the Blitz skies. He had one of the toughest jobs in the emergency services. Seymour and his stretcher partner looked after the dead at incidents, identifying and transporting their remains to the local coroner's office. They helped to save the living as well, pitching in with rescue teams whenever they could, searching through the rubble of toppled buildings for survivors.

On the evening of October 13, 1940, Seymour was having a snack at an ambulance depot housed in the gymnasium of a North London school. There was a raid in progress and the men on duty were trying to drown out the roar of the attack by singing and thumping away at an old piano. But Seymour could still hear the thunder of the London anti-aircraft artillery barrage over their crooning. A week after the September 7 raid, the army had moved hundreds of heavy anti-aircraft ack-ack guns to the capital. Across the city's parks and squares there were new concrete emplacements to house them, ringed with barbed wire, guards and sandbags. Lighter *Bofor* guns were mounted on trucks or trailers and soldiers drove them at breakneck speeds to any areas under attack.

The noise all these guns produced was incredible. But Londoners cheered when they first heard it. They'd been longing for someone to hit back at the Luftwaffe. It didn't matter that very few British shells went anywhere near an enemy plane, although this improved in the later stages of the Blitz. In fact, the ack-ack probably injured thousands of civilians, as gravity meant that any shrapnel or unexploded shells all thundered back to earth in a shower of steel. But most people found the presence of the guns comforting. Their growl became another instrument in the air raid orchestra, joining the sirens, bomb blasts and grinding drone of the attack planes. Anyone who couldn't sleep through all this racket could always shelter underground. It was as quiet as a church crypt down in the tube.

Suddenly, the men stopped singing and the piano was silent. Seymour heard the shrill whistle of a bomb hurtling towards the depot. He threw himself to the floor, remembering the grim Blitz joke that you never heard the bomb that had your name on it. The next instant, the walls shook and the ground trembled with the force of a huge explosion. When Seymour had dusted himself down and recovered his wits, he realized the bomb must have landed only a few streets away. The yard around the depot was covered in torn paper, bits of brick and other debris thrown up by the blast. Minutes later, a warden was bringing an agitated man through the gates.

"The tube station's been hit," the man cried. "People are trapped down there."

Ambulance squads were used to hearing exaggerated damage reports from shocked civilians. Seymour decided the man must be concussed or confused. He couldn't imagine how a surface explosion could have damaged the tube. Then an order came through from district headquarters: every available squad was needed at Bounds Green station. Something terrible had happened in one of the railway tunnels.

When Seymour turned into Bounds Green Road, he saw a large crowd around the entrance of the tube. They stood gawping as dozens of casualties were lifted out on stretchers. Seymour stopped a passing policeman for information. A single German bomb – the same one Seymour had heard falling – had been the cause. It had landed on a row of grand houses further along the road, demolishing two of them. But it didn't explode until it had drilled through the foundations of the buildings. The blast was forced downwards, towards the tunnel. As the tunnel roof cracked open, a great avalanche of mud and clay had swept over the hundreds of people sheltering along the railway platform.

Seymour could see that the station was already busy with rescuers, so he ran towards the terrace of houses to offer his help. He could hardly believe the sight that met his eyes, only a few hundred yards up the road. In place of the elegant buildings, there was nothing but a huge, barren crater. It was dotted with piles of broken furniture, twisted metal pipes and crumbled bricks. Seymour noticed the beam of a light, flickering at the bottom of the crater. Two burly policemen were working in the pit, tugging desperately at a pile of splintered floorboards. He picked his way over to them and introduced himself as an ambulance man.

"There's a lady trapped down there," replied one of the policemen. "You can see the yellow sweater she's wearing. But we can't reach her."

The man held his flashlight to the mouth of a rough tunnel that had formed in all the blast debris. Seymour peered in and saw the body of a young woman, a few yards down, lying in what must have been the cellar of a house.

"I might be able to squeeze in there," he said boldly. "I'm thinner than you two."

"I'll hang on to your legs," the policeman offered. "But be careful. This opening could collapse at any moment."

Seymour ducked headfirst into the hole and began crawling forward. The sweat was soon streaming into his eyes and his lungs were choking on brick dust and gas fumes. He wasn't surprised to smell the gas. Most bomb-sites had problems with gas or water leaks, seeping from smashed utility pipes. Sometimes, when a team of diggers had been working for hours to reach a buried room, they would arrive too late, to find the occupants gassed or drowned. Rescuers regularly worked with the bombs dropping around them, racing against time.

Seymour inched his way towards the cellar, with the walls of the crater tunnel creaking around him. When he'd wriggled close enough to touch the woman's face, he pinched her cheek to test for any signs of life. As he'd feared, she didn't react. Seymour called to the policemen to pull him back out.

Gasping for air, he arrived on the surface to find a team from the Heavy Rescue service at work in the crater. Once he'd told their senior officer about the woman in the cellar, he scrambled out of the bomb site, making for the road. There was a man waiting there, hidden in the shadows.

"I'm looking for my wife," cried the man. "Have you seen her? She was wearing a yellow top."

Seymour shuddered and told him there was little chance of finding anyone alive under all the rubble.

"And what about my daughter?" asked the man in a whisper. "She lived in the house too."

Seymour tried to describe the wrecked tangle of wood and brick he'd crawled through below the crater. But the husband was too dazed to understand. His whole world had been ripped away by one rogue bomb falling out of the darkness. Seymour led him to a warden's post and asked the officer there to look after him. There was nothing more to be done – for the man or his family. He had lost everything, but at least he was safe. Seymour wanted to get back to the tube, to see if other lives were still at risk.

He hurried along the road and reported to the Incident Officer who was managing the rescue operation. In the darkness of the blackout these men carried small blue lamps, so rescuers could always identify them and receive instructions.

"We need your mortuary team down in the tube," the officer told him. "Get moving."

Even with the air raid at its height, the streets around the station were packed with rescue teams, police squads and onlookers. Seymour had to push his way through a crowd to reach the mortuary van – a converted butcher's truck – where his partner was waiting. The two men collected their equipment and hurried into the station's ticket hall.

Riding down on the tube escalator, Seymour passed scores of wounded civilians being helped to the surface. When he reached the underground hall leading to the platforms he saw an emergency medical tent where the injured were receiving treatment. As he approached the platform, everything struck him as very orderly and calm. But, as he turned the corner, Seymour walked straight into a solid pack of shouting, red-faced men, from every branch of the rescue services. Glancing over their heads, he saw a huge mound of black earth and rocks lit by emergency spotlights. It was a terrible sight.

A wall of mud and rubble had piled up on the tracks and spilled across the platform to block the tunnel. He could hear people screaming from the far side of the mound, their cries echoing off the tiled walls and ringing in his ears. Rescue workers swarmed all over, tearing at the soil with bleeding fingers. They were too afraid to use picks and shovels, in case they struck a buried body.

Seymour suddenly realized why so many people had been crowded around the entrance to the platform. There was simply no more room for them at the face of the earth mound where the survivors were trapped. In the narrow space of the tunnel, the rescuers worked in a hot, airless and claustrophobic atmosphere. And more earth could come crashing down on them at any second.

Even though the platform was teeming with people, Seymour began pushing his way forward. He was determined to see if he could do anything to help, before returning to the depot. As he got closer to the mound of earth, he began noticing heads and limbs poking from its surface. The cave-in had happened so quickly, the people sheltering along this section of the tunnel had been buried alive. Rescuers frantically hauled the survivors from the mud, gently explaining to those who were still trapped that they would have to wait their turn to be freed.

Suddenly, Seymour spotted a man standing alone in the swarm of rescuers. From his broad back and powerful physique, Seymour recognized him as another officer from the depot. He was one of the toughest men in the service. Although he'd seen the worst the Blitz had to offer, he'd never made any show of emotion. But this new bomb had brought out some tenderness in the man. Clutched tight in his arms was a small girl who'd been dragged from the clay, bleeding and terrified.

As he stepped closer, Seymour heard him cooing and whispering to the girl, trying to comfort her with soft words and rhymes. The sight of such gentleness in a grizzled Blitz veteran stopped Seymour in his tracks.

"Over here," someone cried out. "Lend a hand."

The man calling was so covered in grime and blood it took Seymour a few seconds to recognize him. He was Dr. Malcolm Manson, a surgeon from the local hospital, standing knee-deep in the mound as he treated the injured. Manson was famed for his cool thinking in the face of an air raid. His face and clothes might have been filthy, but he'd lost none of his authority or determination.

"Take those people to the surface," he ordered. Seymour turned to see a line of stretchers carrying corpses, running along the wall of the platform. They made a grim sight, but Seymour braced himself and got on with the task.

The climb up to the mortuary van was exhausting, amid all the heat and chaos. It took four trips from the platform before Seymour and his partner were ready to drive to the hospital. Riding in the cabin of the van, they tried to rest their aching bodies and frazzled nerves. Seymour had already been on duty for 20 hours, and his work at the underground station was only beginning. He returned twice with the mortuary van, and was then sent across to the ruined line of houses, where the bodies of the woman and her daughter had finally been recovered.

When he'd finished tending to the dead, Seymour hurried back to the rescue effort in the tube. He searched for Dr. Manson and found him still working.

"There's no room for you to help with the digging,"

the doctor told him, when Seymour offered to help. "But you could try to comfort some of the survivors."

Dozens of people were still trapped. Seymour sat with them, chatting and trying to reassure them that help was close at hand. All along the tunnel, heavy rescue workers were digging and fitting wooden props to reinforce the shattered roof. After three hours of horror and panic, it looked as though the disaster was finally being brought under control.

Then there was a sudden scream: *Run for it*. Seymour heard a rumbling sound above him, a movement in the earth. He turned his head and saw Dr. Manson struggling to free a man from a hole in the mound. The doctor looked up for a second, but he ignored the warning, turning back to the man he was attempting to rescue. The next instant a great rush of clay and rock had crashed down from the roof, burying him completely.

Seymour and another man scrambled over to the fresh fall of earth and began digging frantically. After several, desperate seconds they found the doctor's feet and managed to haul him out. He was bruised and bleeding, and two bones in his back had been fractured, but minutes later, he'd regained enough strength to return to work. The following year he was awarded the George Medal for his bravery – next only to the George Cross for gallantry shown by a civilian. Less than a thousand people received this medal during the whole of the Second World War.

The new avalanche had left huge heaps of fresh earth strewn across the top of the mound. Manson and his fellow helpers decided there was little chance of finding anyone else alive in the tunnel. They began scaling down the rescue mission, sending their men home to rest, or out to other Blitz incidents. Seymour managed to steal a few hours of sleep back at his depot, but he was back on duty again when the sirens began wailing in the early evening. For the next three months, Seymour was called out almost every night, a brave defender in the siege of London.

There were 17 people killed in the Bounds Green explosion, but it was only one of several disasters to strike the London Underground during the Blitz. 19 died at Marble Arch when a bomb forced its way through a gap between two steel girders. There were 68 deaths at Balham, many from drowning after the mains water pipes burst, and another 56 people lost their lives at Bank station, when a bomb crashed down an escalator tunnel. These freak explosions proved that there was nowhere in the capital that was completely safe from the bombers. Even in the Underground, there was no escape from the Blitz.

BOMBER'S MOON

*This German Heinkel He-111 was
one of the bombers used extensively
against Britain during the Blitz.*

At 19:00, on November 14, 1940, four men gathered
as usual and began making preparations for the night
ahead. They were a voluntary firefighting team, charged
with protecting one of England's oldest and grandest
buildings: St Michael's Cathedral, Coventry. The local
people had worshipped here for over 600 years. Its tall,
slender spire was a reassuring sight on the city skyline, a
symbol of order and tradition in a world rocked by war.
The men were determined to keep their cathedral safe,
whatever the cost.

At first glance, they seemed an unlikely fire patrol.

Their leader was the cathedral's provost, 56-year-old Richard Howard. Howard was a sensitive, thoughtful man and popular among the local community. Second in command was Jock Forbes, the stonemason and cathedral caretaker. He knew every corner of the huge medieval building, but at 65 years old he was slowing down a bit. The other members of the team made up for this. They were two young men who thought nothing of clambering all over the cathedral's high, lead roof and along its old oak beams.

But the cathedral defenders were already seasoned firefighters. Coventry was home to some of the most important engineering factories in the country and this made it a tempting target for long-range attacks by the Luftwaffe. The first small raids, on the outskirts of the city, came in June. By September, the air raid sirens were wailing almost every evening. Wardens used to joke, "Jerry's late tonight," when the bombers didn't come.

Even so, nobody expected a really big raid. Coventry was located in the heart of the country, hidden far inland and surrounded by open land that was hard to navigate from the air. There was no shimmering river, like the Thames twisting into London, to guide German aircrews to their target. A few lucky bombers might find their way in, but most local people thought it would be impossible to mount a large, coordinated attack.

The cathedral team carefully checked the buckets of sand, hand pumps and blankets, which they used to smother small fires. There was little they could do about damage from high explosives, so their chief mission was to watch for flames spreading from other buildings and to extinguish incendiaries – firebombs. The Germans sometimes dropped scores of these weapons in the hope they would set fire to factories and warehouses. They took the form of short tubes and weighed two kilos (nearly 5lbs). Each one was packed with inflammable chemicals and was designed to smash through slates and tiles and lodge in roof spaces before igniting.

Once they'd flared into life, they burned so fiercely that they could melt through steel. The surest way to put them out was to cover them in sand or soil. Some incendiaries could be smothered or dunked in liquid, but if they contained the chemical mixture called thermite they would continue burning even underwater. To make life harder for fire teams and wardens, the Germans fitted explosives to around one in ten of these weapons. Blitz defenders were never sure if an incendiary would blow up in their face as they struggled to put it out.

At 19:10 the first sirens began their spine-chilling howl. Ten minutes later, provost Howard spotted around a dozen German planes approaching the city. They were Heinkel He-111 bombers dropping parachute flares.

"They won't be needing those fireflies," moaned Jock, pointing up to the sky. "Moon's so bright tonight I could read my paper by it."

Howard looked along the high roof of his cathedral. The lead that covered it was dusted in white frost, glistening like snow in the brightest full moon he'd seen for months. "That's a bomber's moon," Howard agreed with his friend. "Let's hope it's only a light raid tonight."

But the provost and his cathedral were facing an explosive firestorm. Less than an hour later, he and his men would be caught up in one of the biggest air raids of the Blitz.

On November 11, British Intelligence had received a shocking report from one of their agents. A German prisoner of war – or POW – had revealed that the Luftwaffe was assembling a great armada of bombers to attack a city in the Midlands. It would be Birmingham, Wolverhampton or Coventry, but he didn't know which. The raid was scheduled to coincide with the next full moon, around November 14/15. People in the Blitz dreaded these bomber's moons, as the extra light they gave off helped German pilots to drop their bombs more accurately. Intelligence officers were still questioning the reliability of the POW's claims when they received a note from Bletchley Park, home of the *Enigma Machine* codebreakers.

The Enigma was a portable, typewriter-sized device used by the German armed forces to send coded messages. It scrambled words into a complex series of random letters. British and Polish mathematicians had been studying versions of the machine since its invention by a firm of German engineers in the 1920s, and they were able to decipher some of their opponents' secret messages. The information they provided was codenamed ULTRA, and it was invaluable to the Allied forces throughout the war.

The ULTRA report made clear that the Luftwaffe was indeed planning a massive raid, codenamed *Moonlight Sonata Corn*. A staggering 500 bombers were being made ready for the raid, to strike at one of England's major industrial cities. The Bletchley team had also learned that the raid was in direct response to an RAF bomber attack on Munich, on November 8. Hitler was furious that the British had dared to threaten the city where his beloved Nazi party was founded. He had been visiting Munich himself, only hours before the raid, bragging about the party's achievements at a public meeting.

ULTRA had other clues about the German attack. Luftwaffe technicians had been ordered to a group of radio stations dotted along the coast of occupied France. Each station could transmit a powerful radio beam deep into British airspace. At least one of these mysterious beams was being configured to pass directly over the rooftops of Coventry.

Some RAF officers always believed that German pilots in the Blitz relied on 'dead reckoning' for their navigation. This technique involved calculating wind strength and aircraft speed, then looking for landmarks along the route to check their position. But, in reality, the Germans had access to sophisticated guidance systems. By listening to a regular beeping pulse in their headsets, bomber crews could follow a broad radio beam that led them directly to their targets. British scientists soon realized what the Germans were up to, and they tried to disrupt the beams by broadcasting their own counterfeit signals. These worked successfully, luring many German crews off course.

By the time of the *Moonlight Sonata* raid, however, the Luftwaffe had developed the *X-Gerät* system – the X-gadget. Like many German codenames, the word itself contained a clue to its real meaning. Beams from several transmitters crossed over a first, narrow beam, making different sounds that a pilot could listen for using an onboard radio set. When pilots heard the sound of a new beam, they could tell how far they were from their target. X-Gerät beams crossed at precise distances along the bomber's flight path. By pushing a button when they heard the beep of each beam, pilots could ready, prime and release their bombs to drop with astonishing accuracy.

The British were still trying to understand the principles behind X-Gerät in mid-November 1940. They knew it depended on a new type of radio set being fitted into each bomber, and they had even captured one from a German wreck in the Channel. But the mysterious device was still sitting on a navy scientist's desk, waterlogged and full of sand, on the afternoon of November 14. In *Operation Headache*, the RAF tried their best to disrupt the invisible beams they suspected were slicing across English skies, putting up the usual counterfeit radio signals. They also launched *Operation Cold Water*, ordering air raids against radio stations in France and sending a

squadron of night fighters to patrol the skies over the
Midlands. But these countermeasures couldn't prevent
the Germans from getting through. As soon as dusk
fell in France, 13 *Heinkel* bombers, from the elite
Kampfgruppe 100 Pathfinder squadron, were droning
towards Coventry, following X-Gerät beams. They
released flares, high explosives and 10,000 firebombs
over the city, marking out the target for the main
attack force. Hundreds of German bombers were
approaching from the south. Their crews saw the fires
dancing on the horizon, and set a course for the heart
of the blaze.

At 20:00, Howard and his men were watching the
city burning around them. In the first minutes of the
raid, they'd taken some comfort from the fact there
were no more than a dozen or so enemy bombers in
the night sky. But when it became clear that this force
was only lighting the way, they realized the cathedral
was in terrible danger. The four men watched as a
great swarm of twin-engined Heinkels massed above
them, their bombs streaking down in what looked like
a hailstorm of steel.

The first incendiaries hit the church in three places
at once: on the roof above the choir stalls, inside the
main hall among the pews, and on the roof above the
organ. Howard and his men rushed into action. They
covered the bomb on the stalls with sand and heaved
it over the cathedral battlements. Down among the
pews, the other bomb was hissing and spitting white

81

sparks. Howard had to empty two buckets of sand over it to subdue the flames. The organ bomb was even harder to deal with. It had melted through the lead on the roof and clattered onto the oak ceiling below. They ripped away the roof covering to get at the bomb, dumping sand into the jagged opening, their faces flashing white and crimson as they battled with it. When Howard was satisfied that they'd finally put it out, he pumped gallons of water into the roof space, to quell the fire that was crackling in the beams.

But there was no time to rest. The air raid was still gaining momentum, with new ranks of bombers arriving to replace others returning to France. All around the cathedral, high explosives and fires were reducing the old city to rubble and ash. Another two firebombs struck the cathedral roof. The flames fizzed white-hot, splitting the lead and falling among the old oak beams.

The cathedral firefighters managed to extinguish them both but, the next instant, four more bombs thudded into the roof. Before the men could reach them, three of the burning tubes melted through the lead. There was a shout from the floor of the main church: "The ceiling's on fire."

Howard watched the smoke billowing through the holes. His men had dealt with the fourth incendiary, but the other charges had started a powerful blaze.

"We need some help to tackle this one," Howard told his friends. "We're almost out of sand and water.

See if you can get a message to the fire station."

One of the team rushed to the side of the roof and began shouting down to the street below. The lane was thick with smoke and glowing red with fire, but luckily, a passing policeman heard the calls for help. He rushed to a nearby police station and asked the desk sergeant to contact the fire control office.

"There's not a pump to spare," the operator told the sergeant. "We've got over 200 fires to deal with. I'll send someone when I can."

It wasn't until 21:30 that a fire truck arrived outside the cathedral, manned by an auxiliary – volunteer – crew who had driven from the suburbs of Birmingham. It was one of hundreds of fire teams who came from all over the Midlands to help Coventry that night. Howard was overjoyed when he saw the firemen unpacking their equipment. The blaze in the roof was burning fiercely, but it might not be too late to save the cathedral.

He watched as the crew stretched a length of hose up the staircase of the cathedral spire and began playing water across the flames. But suddenly, the pipe went limp in their hands. There wasn't enough mains pressure to get a steady flow to the roof. A moment later, the water supply failed completely. The firemen tried hooking their pumps to another fire hydrant, but this too was mysteriously dry.

"What's happened?" cried Howard, as the men hurried to find another hydrant.

"The mains water supply has gone," one of them cried. "The German bombs must have blown it up."

After three hours of bombing, the raid still hadn't reached its ferocious climax. Of the 552 aircraft that took off from France that night, 449 made their way successfully to Coventry, each with a potential bomb load of 2,000 kilos (4,400lbs). There had never been an assault like it and it continued until 06:00 the following day. Approaching pilots spotted the city wreathed in flames from over a hundred miles away. The blaze was so intense the German crews could smell the foul plume of fire and smoke they'd created as they circled at an altitude of 3km (10,000 feet).

Cowering in basement shelters, Andersons and factory cellars, the local people were bewildered by the scale of the raid. The Luftwaffe dropped over 30,000 incendiaries that night, in a deliberate attempt to start an all-consuming firestorm. Temperatures in the heart of the blaze were hot enough to melt bricks. To help spread the fires from building to building, the Germans used high explosives, scattering blazing material far and wide. They also released a fearsome weapon known as a parachute mine, which could obliterate whole rows of houses in a single enormous blast.

Bigger than a coffin, the jet-black tube of a parachute mine drifted silently to earth under its silk canopy. Some people thought these parachutes must belong to enemy airmen who'd bailed out of stricken planes. They ran towards the fluttering white shapes, eager to get their hands on the men destroying their city. But they were in for a terrible surprise.

Originally manufactured for the *Kriegsmarine* – the German Navy – the parachute mine could be dropped in shallow waters for use against enemy shipping. Packed with 1,000 kilos (2,200lbs) of explosive, the mine sat on the seabed until the motion of a passing ship triggered it to go off. But the Luftwaffe exploited the awesome power of the mine for use as a Blitz weapon too. It drifted slowly during its descent, so the bomb casing didn't crash deep into the ground before exploding. Parachute mines literally flattened any surface building, wiping out whole residential blocks. Anyone caught within a few hundred yards of the explosion was killed. Wardens in Coventry discovered the bodies of civilians lying around the perimeter of a parachute mine crater. Their flesh and clothes were unmarked, but their internal organs had been crushed by the hurricane-force of the bomb blast. The Germans dropped 50 of these mines on Coventry that night and continued to use them throughout the Blitz.

The city's defenders were unable to make much impact on the massive, mauling fleet of Heinkels. With their 24 heavy ack-ack guns and a mobile force of 12 Bofor guns they were only prepared for light to medium raids. In addition to the artillery, a few factories had permission to mount machine guns on their walls. Although these guns managed to keep up a solid barrage throughout the raid, they only managed to bring down a single German aircraft.

Coventry also had 56 barrage balloons. They were around 20m (65 feet) long and full of hydrogen, and could be winched up into the sky at the end of thick, steel cables designed to snag and destroy low-flying aircraft. Although they didn't hook any planes that night, they did protect the city from strafing – machine gun attacks by dive bombers. London was screened by over 400 of these silver balloons.

As for the night fighters, it was almost impossible for them to engage the enemy. British pilots could see the bombers, caught in the white beam of searchlights or glinting in the moonlight, but they would lose sight of them the next second as they slipped into the darkness.

If the raid had taken place a few months later, it could have been a different story. British scientists had just developed a new weapon in the air war – Airborne Interception Radar, or AI. An onboard radar system allowed fighter pilots to track and destroy unsuspecting aircraft. But the system was still being tested and had only been installed in a small number of fighters. AI was a closely guarded secret, which the RAF protected by explaining to British newspapers that their pilots' night vision improved dramatically with a diet of carrots.

Coventry had been selected as Hitler's revenge attack for the Munich raid because it was at the heart of Britain's war industries. Famous in Victorian times for the skills of its watchmakers and bicycle designers, the factory workers of 1940 manufactured complex engine parts and other precision instruments. But Coventry had an unusual – even unfortunate – street layout. Because of the way the medieval town had developed over the centuries, large factories and terraced houses stood side by side. Planners had allowed workshops to be built next to grand medieval churches and other monuments. There was no large industrial area on the outskirts of Coventry. This jumble of housing and industry gave Coventry its special character, but it also exposed ordinary people to the horror of the Blitz. German pilots dropped their explosives with amazing accuracy on their industrial targets. But standing only yards away were houses and schools – and a famous cathedral.

Before the Birmingham fire team arrived, the provost had already collected some of the silverware, candlesticks and religious ornaments from inside his church. He carried them carefully to the nearby police station and put them into an underground vault for safe storage.

For the next four hours, Howard stood in the sheltered porch of the police station, watching his beloved cathedral burn to the ground. Without any water for their pumps, the auxiliary firemen were powerless to stop it. The great walls of the church finally collapsed and Howard looked on in silence, as the heart of the cathedral became a raging inferno.

One third of the inner city burned to the ground that night. Despite Howard's best efforts, Coventry's majestic cathedral was lost.

There was no all-clear signal given on the morning of November 15. The sirens had either been blasted to pieces or had no power supply for their electric motors. The gas, water and electricity services for the city were in disarray. Around 06:30, wardens began hurrying through the shell-holed streets, calling to people in their shelters that the raid was finally over. Coventry had a civilian population of roughly 200,000. They came up to the surface to find their beautiful city a smoking ruin. Crowds wandered through the blasted landscape, crunching their way through a thick carpet of broken glass, ash and brick. The fires had consumed hundreds of buildings and damaged 70% of the city's factories. People described bizarre sights and smells in the aftermath of the blaze. A cloud of cigar smoke hung around a charred tobacco stand; sides of pork and beef were stacked in a butcher's shop, perfectly roasted.

Over the following days, rescue workers and army units poured into the area, digging survivors out from under the rubble and trying to get the production lines moving again. Although thousands fled to the countryside, fearing another air raid, most people didn't give up on their battered city. They returned to work and tried to rebuild their lives.

From the Luftwaffe's perspective, the attack was a stunning success. An officer in the German propaganda service even coined a new word celebrating the attack: *Coventrieren* – to Coventrate – was to flatten a city by aerial bombardment. But the Germans were foolish to crow about their achievements. Coventry's engineering output was restored within a few weeks, and the raid taught the RAF valuable lessons about incendiaries. They used them to inflict devastating attacks on German cities, later in the war.

A total of 568 people died in the Coventry raid and 863 were injured. In May 1962, their lives were remembered as part of a special service held to open the city's new cathedral. This bold, modern building was constructed next to the preserved ruins of the old cathedral. The provost, Richard Howard, was there, of course, leading the proceedings.

In recent years, Coventry has become widely involved in international peace initiatives. The city is twinned with Dresden and Volgograd (formerly Stalingrad) and other cities whose civilians suffered hugely in wars. Coventry hosts its own Peace Month each year, organizing a season of talks and exhibitions. The new cathedral plays host to many of these events. Bruised and bloodied as it was in the Blitz, Coventry had refused to die.

A DANGEROUS PROFESSION

A bomb warden waits for the disposal team to arrive.

Lieutenant Robert Davies glanced up at the mighty dome of St. Paul's Cathedral towering above him. Standing 111m (365 feet) high, and supported by walls of dazzling white stone, the dome was one of London's most striking architectural treasures. St. Paul's itself was a national landmark, rich in history. Admiral Horatio Nelson, the Duke of Wellington and the building's great architect, Sir Christopher Wren, were all buried inside its crypt. This was the fourth cathedral to occupy the site since the Saxons first built a holy place there in the year 604. The other three had been destroyed in wars or consumed by fire – the last in the Great Fire of London, in 1666.

Lieutenant Davies was well aware of the building's long and violent history, and now the cathedral was threatened with destruction once again. It was the middle of the afternoon, but the usually busy streets around St. Paul's were deserted. Every building, shop and office space had been cleared. Davis was alone inside the police cordon. At his feet was a large, gaping hole in the road. At the bottom of this hole, a huge unexploded German bomb was lodged next to the cathedral's foundations. The bomb was alive, and ticking. Davies was the man who'd been given the job of defusing this monster. The future of London's cathedral rested in his trembling hands.

Before the declaration of war in 1939, the British government hadn't paid much attention to the problems posed by unexploded bombs, or UXBs. Although there had been instances of civilian bombing in Spain and the first Blitzkrieg strikes, officials had simply assumed that any explosives dropped from an airplane would blow up, or detonate, on impact with the ground. But they were quite wrong. Around one in ten of all the high-explosive bombs used in the Blitz became UXBs. Teams of 'sappers' (army engineers) and bomb disposal experts were hastily assembled to locate each one and make them safe.

The government's first response to the UXB threat was optimistic, to say the least. They assumed that wardens and other civilian volunteers would simply pick up the bombs where they landed and carry them to areas of open ground cordoned off by the police, known as *bomb cemeteries*. There, the explosive chemicals inside the bomb canister could be removed or detonated harmlessly. Officials generously decided the wardens might need some special training for this. In the meantime, they asked soldiers from the Royal Engineers to take care of potential UXBs.

In the opening months of the phoney war, many generals doubted whether a single bomb would ever smash into British soil. But they bowed to the government's wishes and in early November 1939 began forming special Bomb Disposal Parties. These were teams of three men – a corporal and two sappers – armed with shovels, a small truck and some sandbags. In case they didn't like the idea of loading a bomb onto their truck, they were taught how to plant explosives around its casing. Then they could blow it up where they'd found it. The army assumed that most UXBs would be found lying on their sides on the ground. But early Luftwaffe bombing raids soon proved them to be mistaken.

The first German bomb to strike British soil landed on a remote field in the Shetland Islands, on November 13, 1939. A lone rabbit was the only casualty, which may have inspired the wartime song *Run Rabbit Run*. The islands were an important target for the Germans because the Royal Navy and Royal Air Force had tactical bases there. Following another raid in late December, RAF inspectors came across some strange holes in the ground. They dug down, following a slanting tunnel, and discovered several small UXBs. The inspectors were amazed to discover that each one of the explosive canisters was fitted with a complex and deadly fuse.

Lieutenant Davies stared into the great pit of mud and clay at the foot of the cathedral. The bomb had smashed into the ground at two in the morning, three days earlier, during a particularly heavy air raid. Davies and his men reached the scene within an hour. They had been working non-stop, just to get down to the buried weapon. On the first day, three of the team had disturbed a broken gas main near the surface and had been injured. It took a full day to shut down the local gas supply and resume the excavation.

They'd first sighted their quarry 5m (16 feet) down, and realized they were dealing with a dreaded *Hermann*, a reference to the portly Luftwaffe commander, Hermann Goering. The Hermann was a powerful bomb, weighing 1,000 kilos (2,200lbs). It was easily capable of destroying the cathedral and the office buildings nearby. Around 55% of its enormous weight was made up of a pure explosive called trinitrotoluene, or TNT. Only the gargantuan *Satan bomb* was larger, weighing 1,500 kilos (3,300lbs).

As the men examined their find, the walls of the pit groaned and the bomb suddenly lurched forwards, dropping another 4m (13 feet) through a layer of wet clay. The team had to begin digging again, but first they had a shocking discovery to report. One of them had managed to sneak a look at the bomb's fuse, mounted in what was called the pocket on the side of the casing. Amazingly, every German fuse was stamped with a serial code and a number, indicating the type of mechanism found inside. The Hermann was fitted with a No.17 fuse. This time-delay device could be set to detonate the bomb at any point between impact and 72 hours later. If the fuse was undamaged, Davies had almost run out of time.

By the summer of 1940, the British government was beginning to get the picture about UXBs. Luftwaffe raids were getting heavier and more frequent, leaving behind thousands of dormant explosives. The three-man bomb parties were overwhelmed and to nobody's surprise there were very few volunteers coming forward to join them. To make matters worse, the fuses discovered on Shetland suggested that bomb disposal was going to be a skilled and extremely dangerous business.

Government ministers scrapped their civilian recruitment campaign and asked the army to form 24 bomb disposal sections, each made up of an officer, a sergeant and 14 soldiers. By the end of the Blitz, there were 220 sections working flat out. The Royal Engineers supplied most of the men, many of whom had a background in specialist trades such as demolition or mining. They were equipped with the usual trucks, sandbags and plenty of picks and shovels. Another lesson from the Shetlands was that UXBs weren't going to be sitting around on the surface. The disposal sections would have to do a lot of digging.

The first rule of dealing with a UXB was simple: you have to find the thing before you can make it safe. Out in a Shetland field it had been hard enough to spot the bombs' entry holes. But in a busy city district, with regular air raids and other distractions, locating a small hole could take hours of searching. The Royal Engineers soon discovered that UXBs were never located directly below the entry hole. Falling at great speed, they twisted and veered through the soil, changing course when they struck buried objects such as rocks and pipes.

The bomb sections had to calculate the angle of a UXB's path through the ground and then dig towards it. These digs could turn into major excavations. In soft ground, they sometimes had to burrow 18m (60 feet) to get to their bomb. They shored up the pit with anything they could find. Sawn timber was in short supply, so they pillaged the wreckage of air-raid sites, searching for front doors, floorboards and strips of corrugated steel from ruined Andersons.

When the team finally revealed the bomb casing, glass smooth after its long journey through the earth, they clambered out of the pit. From that point on, as few men as possible worked around the bomb. The most experienced engineer – usually the officer – stood alone next to the casing. His first task was to locate the fuse. It was a heart-stopping moment.

Whatever number he saw printed there could decide whether he lived or died.

It was a common sight during the Blitz to see a street cordoned off, with a policeman standing in front of the sign: DANGER UXB. Not far away, a lone bomb disposal expert would be crouching next to the explosive canister, considering his next move. The battle to disable the bomb depended on cracking the riddle of its fuse. And the Luftwaffe's fuses were the most intricate in the world.

German designers had pioneered the use of electrical fuses in munitions, believing them to be more efficient than the mechanical detonators used by their enemies. Their research had been going on for years, even in peacetime. If the British authorities had bothered to check, they would have found the Luftwaffe's fuse designs had been registered at the London Patent Office since 1932.

Although bombs were packed with deadly explosives such as TNT, these materials were surprisingly stable. The sudden impact with the ground wasn't enough to detonate the explosive. Instead, a smaller charge needed to be planted inside the canister – a bomb inside a bomb. This could be set off by a controlled spark, causing a chain reaction that would end with a massive blast.

Each German bomb had a circular chamber running through it, packed with pellets made from an explosive more volatile than TNT. Nestling among them was the fuse, its head visible in the outside bomb casing. When the bomb was released from its rack inside the plane, the fuse was given a sudden jolt of electricity. It took a split second for this to pass through the device, powering it up, by which time the bomb had dropped a safe distance from the plane. Now it was armed and dangerous.

In the simplest fuse, the No.15, a trembler switch clicked into place when the bomb hit the ground. This released the stored electricity, and the fuse fired a spark into the explosive pellets, detonating the TNT. But, if the switch failed or the fuse was defective in some other way, the bomb drilled into the earth and became a UXB.

By stripping and testing some of the UXBs that had been hauled out of the Shetland field, RAF scientists quickly spotted a weakness in the design of the No.15. It was easy to drain the electric charge out of it, by depressing two plungers on the head of the fuse. Once the fuse was disarmed, there was no chance of the bomb exploding. The sapper could either cut a hole in the steel casing and pump or dig out the explosive without moving the bomb, or transport it intact to the nearest cemetery. Teams still had the nerve-wracking job of handling the fuse and twisting it out from the bomb casing.

But one RAF engineer soon developed a simple tool for this job, known as a *Crabtree*. A sapper screwed his Crabtree into position over the fuse and tied a length of string to the top of it. When he was safely tucked away behind a wall of sandbags, he yanked on the string. The Crabtree depressed the plungers, then levered the fuse out.

Bomb disposal teams were always sharing secrets, tips and tactics with one another. But the Germans were learning new tricks too. When a sapper came across a mysterious No. 25 fuse in a UXB he'd dismantled, he rushed it to the weapons experts. They discovered that the Germans had created a new fuse that would detonate if anything touched the plungers. So sappers quickly modified their Crabtrees to get around this threat.

The Luftwaffe responded with the No. 50 fuse – a booby trap for British sappers. This was a trembler switch that would detonate the bomb at the slightest movement. In a deadly game of cat and mouse with the German designers, British disposal teams came up with the idea of pumping a thick, sticky liquid into the No. 50. Once this had gummed up the works, they could tackle the fuse without worrying that the trembler switch would suddenly activate. But this was a more difficult job than it sounds. Bombs were often partly hidden in mud or debris and rolling or dragging them into a better position was out of the question.

Crude as these techniques might sound, they allowed sappers to disable the majority of UXBs. But disposal work was still dangerous. At the height of the Blitz, a sapper's life expectancy was only ten weeks.

Some died even when they took every precaution, and weapons experts began to worry that the Germans might have developed a new, deadlier fuse. In August, 1940, their fears were confirmed. A sapper sent them something he'd recovered from a badly damaged bomb: it was the No.17, a time-delay fuse.

Davies slowly lowered himself into the pit below St. Paul's Cathedral. Even though newspaper reports had been censored, to prevent the Germans from using the bomb as a propaganda tool, he knew there were whispers going around London that the building was in peril. Robert Davies was an easy-going, veteran soldier. Born in Cornwall, he'd emigrated to Canada as a young man and served with the Canadian Army during the First World War. But, despite all his years as a man of action, his nerves were tingling as he climbed down towards the Hermann, bedded in the clay. It felt as though the eyes of the city were looking down on him, watching his every move.

Davies knew that there was only one way to beat an undamaged No.17 fuse. Designed to cause maximum disruption to civilian and military life, these time-delay UXBs were fitted with a clock that counted down the hours before their detonation. All UXBs had to be left undisturbed for three days after they were first discovered – until they either exploded or the fuse proved to be defective. But an inventor at the General Electric Company had built a machine that could stop the No.17's clock – a huge magnet that immobilized its hands. It was a large and unwieldy object, the shape of a horse collar and as heavy as a man. But it worked. Finally, sappers were able to start disarming No.17s.

Davies stepped over to the side of the massive unexploded bomb. He touched it with his fingertips, very softly. Like all bomb disposal men, he was used to weighing up the risks of each mission. His superiors had classed the St. Paul's bomb as a Grade C. This was the highest of the three risk categories used for UXBs – A was low priority, B could be exploded on site, but a C had to be removed urgently. Davies knew it might take hours to fit the clock-stopper and there was still a chance it wouldn't prevent the bomb from exploding. After all, the fuse might be booby-trapped.

Only ten days earlier, a sapper had discovered a new German gadget hidden inside a No.17 – an anti-withdrawal switch. This could detonate the bomb if it sensed anything tugging at the fuse. Davies wasn't convinced he'd be able to neutralize it in the tight space of the pit. There was something else that was worrying him too, aside from these technical concerns.

Standing next to the imposing bulk of the UXB, he began to sense something evil in the atmosphere around him. It was almost as though he could feel the explosive menace of the bomb, the frenzied rage that was desperate to burst out from its steel cage. Davies sensed that this was a bomb that wanted to explode. So he made a quick decision.

"Sergeant," he called up to the edge of the pit.

"Get some ropes around this thing and find me a truck. We're taking it for a drive."

It took several hours for the bomb team to winch the Hermann to the surface, using pulleys mounted on the back of two trucks. Twice, with a sickening crack, the bomb slipped free from its cables and slid back into the clay pit. On their third attempt, the engineers finally managed to swing it onto the back of a truck. They lashed it in place and wedged cushions, blankets and wooden boards around it to prevent it from rolling. Davies climbed into the driver's seat and dismissed his men. This was one ride he would be taking alone.

London's police cleared the streets for the bomb truck, all the way to the nearest bomb cemetery at Hackney Marshes. They evacuated houses, pubs and shops along the whole length of the route. A police car topped with a red flag set off in the advance, driving half a mile ahead of the bomb truck. Davies followed, as quickly as he dared, anxious not to wake the monster strapped to the bed of the truck.

As they approached their destination, several police cars began circling the streets, warning residents up to a mile away to open their windows. This reduced the risk of glass shattering that was caused by a build-up of air pressure after bomb blasts.

Reaching the heart of the cemetery, Davies and his team carefully unloaded the bomb and set explosive charges around it. Then, when everyone was safe inside a sandbag bunker, he detonated the charges.

There was an earth-shaking rumble all around the cemetery as the Hermann gouged out a crater 2.5m (eight feet) deep and 30m (100 feet) across. The great cathedral of St. Paul's had been saved for the nation.

Davies and his men did not go unrewarded for their daring work. King George VI had been impressed by the courage of the bomb team and scores of other Blitz heroes. The King and Queen themselves had refused to leave Buckingham Palace during the attacks, hoping to set an example of strength and determination for their subjects. Encouraged by Churchill, George VI introduced a new medal to recognize and encourage bravery on the Home Front. On September 30, 1940, Davies and one of his sappers, George Wylie, were awarded the new George Cross. After the Victoria Cross, it remains the second highest award for courage in Great Britain.

Sadly, though, Davies' career ended in disgrace. In 1942 he was imprisoned for 18 months and thrown out of the army, after a sensational court martial. The charges involved fraud and looting from bomb sites. Perhaps the pressure of handling UXBs every day had finally become too much for the quiet Cornishman? Davies emigrated to Australia and vanished. It wasn't until 1970 that he was heard of again, when he put his George Cross up for auction. He died only a few years later.

The Luftwaffe dropped over half a million bombs

on British soil in the course of the war. The bomb disposal sections defused around 50,000 UXBs, and thousands of other explosive and incendiary devices scattered by the enemy. Their courage and hard work at home was the equal of any soldiers on the battlefield.

AN OCEAN OF FIRE

Firefighters struggle to control a blaze.

There were times that night when the fire almost seemed to become a living thing, full of menace and hate. It turned the firemen's jets of water into scalding rain, set their clothes and boots alight, and blinded them with flying embers. Flames flickered and played in the shells of hundreds of burning buildings, sweeping along the narrow lanes and cobbled yards of the old city.

Fireman Henry Burrow was lost in the heart of the blaze, trapped in a long, burning street. Fires crackled all around him, hissing and roaring, sending out swarms of sparks and clouds of acrid, choking smoke. With buildings collapsing on every side, Burrow staggered over piles of brick and rubble, trying to shield his eyes from the searing heat. He was searching for a way out.

But the fire was after him, outpacing and encircling him like an animal hunting down its prey. Every

105

alleyway and road that might have led Burrow to safety was already blocked or ablaze. The flames were 18m (60 feet) high, steadily closing around him, drowning out his hoarse cries for help. Burrow suddenly stumbled and crashed down into the road. He was too exhausted to go on. With the incredible heat burning his lungs and blistering his skin, Burrow lifted his head for a last glance at the fires that were tormenting him. He noticed a flicker of movement almost hidden by the smoke. Rubbing his eyes, he saw the hazy figure of a small boy, standing in a doorway. It was his three-year-old son, waving to him.

Burrow smiled to himself. He'd heard tales of firemen seeing strange things in the swirling confusion of a blaze. But he could think of nothing better than a last chance to say goodbye to his boy, even if the figure was only a trick of his imagination. Burrow looked again. This time, he noticed his son gesturing, pointing into the doorway where he was standing. He wanted his father to come to him. Burrow dragged himself up and made his way over. As he got closer, his son faded into the smoke and the red glow of the fires, but Burrow could see a stairway opening up beyond the doorway. He climbed down the stairs and found himself in a deep cellar; a cool, quiet room. Safe from the inferno raging above ground, he huddled in a corner and closed his eyes to sleep.

Henry Burrow had been caught in one of the worst fires ever to strike central London. It was started at 18:00 on the evening of December 29, 1940 by thousands of German incendiary bombs clattering across the rooftops of the City. The raid itself wasn't particularly heavy for the Blitz – 136 bombers joined the attack, compared to 350 on Black Saturday – and because of a thick fog that was settling around their landing strips in France, the Luftwaffe were under some pressure to finish their mission early. So it only lasted for around three hours, compared to the 11 hours of horror that Coventry had suffered six weeks earlier.

But a number of things combined to fan the blaze into an ocean of fire, destroying a great swathe of London's famous financial district and killing over 170 people, including 16 firemen.

Since the start of the Blitz, Londoners had always suspected that the Luftwaffe liked to give the City a good pasting on Sundays, the day when most offices, schools and public buildings were locked and empty. Without any firewatchers on duty – caretakers or voluntary staff who watched for incendiary bombs – the City was more vulnerable over the weekend.

Blitzed Londoners were getting quite casual about extinguishing incendiaries. These hissing canisters of inflammable chemicals were almost harmless if caught early. But with nobody to stamp them out or report them, they quickly took hold in attics and lofts, spreading their fires into surrounding buildings. It wasn't until January 1941 that the government made it compulsory for firms and offices to employ full-time firewatchers.

Over 9,000 firemen turned out to battle the blaze, moving across acres of burning streets in small teams of three or four. They had 2,000 water pumps at their disposal, but many were useless, as German high explosive bombs had ruptured sections of the capital's water supply at the start of the attack. The firemen had faced this problem before and had come up with the idea of building dozens of huge, canvas water tanks around the City. Once these were drained, the teams turned to the Thames for their water. But when they ran their emergency hoses down to the river on December 29, they were in for a shock.

There was a strong tide out to sea that evening and all that was left in the river was a shallow channel of icy water. Fire teams were forced to wade through thick mud and in many places they couldn't reach the water. They did the best they could to get their hoses to shore, but there weren't enough fireboats to make up for the shortage. In desperation, fire teams ran their hoses into flooded bomb craters and ponds.

But it was the street layout of the old financial district that caused the biggest headaches for the fire teams. The area was famous for its narrow, twisting passageways and crowded offices. Firemen had to track their way through a hellish maze of blazing alleyways walled with tenement buildings four floors high. The fires howled through these streets, raising the air temperature until hose water turned to steam and buildings became so hot they could spontaneously burst into flames.

This was the scene that confronted Henry Burrow, when he first reported for duty at a central fire station near St. Paul's Cathedral.

Burrow and his team were auxiliary firemen, based in the north-western suburb of Hampstead. Like most voluntary fire teams, they had five or six men and had been given small trucks or converted London taxis and trailers to transport themselves and their equipment. Each team had a powerful trailer pump, some hoses, axes and ropes. On the way into town, the firemen had been appalled by the radiant crimson skies hanging over the city. Rows of warehouses along the Thames had started burning and the fire was spreading south of the river. They all knew they had a long night ahead of them.

The streets around the fire station were already ravaged by the blaze. Some had been blocked with mounds of brick from ruined buildings; others were lined with fires burning out of control. But somehow, the team's driver managed to find a way through. Burrow – known as 'Skipper' by his friends – was ordered to take his pump and two water jets to a street only a stone's throw from St. Paul's. The cathedral was ringed with fires, but so far it hadn't been badly damaged. His team had to stop the blaze from jumping across the street and threatening the monument itself.

The men hurried across to their position and soon had the pump hooked up to a hydrant. They were in luck. There was enough water pressure for them to send two tall jets of water cascading into the fire. Although the blaze was well established on three sides, they were managing to hold it back. Three men worked around each hose, taking turns gripping the ice-cold canvas and brass nozzle. The pulsing tube could kick like a horse if it wasn't treated with respect. Soon they were soaking wet.

A few yards away, the road was steaming as the fires evaporated any puddles of water. When a man left the hose for some reason – to tend to the pump or check on his mates – the thick cloth of his uniform dried off in seconds. A fireman was either so cold and wet he lost all feeling in his hands, or so baked by the blaze and clouds of sparks he could be temporarily blinded.

Burrow's team might have beaten the fire that night if their luck hadn't suddenly run out. To shouts of disbelief, their hoses trembled and ran dry as the mains supply failed. Without a constant pressure of water to keep them at bay, the flames roared back into life. There was no time to waste. With the fires gathering strength on every side, the team quickly packed their kit onto the trailer and piled into their makeshift truck. As they rumbled away from the swelling monster of smoke and fire behind them, part of a terrace of office blocks up ahead tottered and collapsed. The road was completely blocked. Worse, a new fire rushed in through the gap in the buildings and stopped the men from trying to clamber to safety over the mound of rubble.

The men jumped down from the truck, and frantically tried to retrace their steps. Although they were heading back towards the first fire, they were hoping to escape down an alleyway or through a bomb-site gap in the terraced buildings. But the street was full of billowing smoke and the flames were getting closer. The air was almost too hot to breathe and the men couldn't see where they were going. One of them fell. Burrow was by his side in a flash, lifting him up and encouraging him to go on. Another man tumbled, choking on thick, black fumes. Burrow heard a scream. He looked up and saw a wash of flaming liquid rushing towards him along the gutters at the side of the road. It was burning oil, either flowing from a broken tank in a ruined building or from an enemy weapon. The Germans had been dropping heavy drums of oil fitted with explosives, hoping they would act as incendiaries.

The oil overwhelmed the terrified group of firemen, setting their boots ablaze and blistering any exposed skin. Burrow looked down and saw that his hands were on fire. Screaming in pain, he smothered the flames and wrapped his arms inside his coat.

"There's no way out," cried another man. "We're trapped in here like rats."

Sydney Henry Burrow had been a mechanic before the Second World War started. He was a firm patriot, so when he saw the advertisements for voluntary

AN OCEAN OF FIRE

firemen posted around fire stations in 1938, he decided to add his name to the lists. London already had a professional fire service of course, with thousands of full-time members, 59 stations and three fireboats. There was a strong sense of community within their ranks and they had a tradition of strict discipline and giving and obeying orders without question. Not surprisingly, the 23,000 volunteers who signed up ruffled a few feathers among these professionals. It took a long time for them to accept the male volunteers into their community, and life was even harder for the thousands of women who joined up. They were usually given the most dreary jobs around the station, such as cleaning and cooking, but some were promoted to become drivers or given more interesting work.

During the phoney war, some bitter Londoners criticized auxiliary firemen as layabouts. Many volunteers refused to wear their uniform in public and thousands resigned or tried to move to another emergency service. This hostility was partly due to the small numbers of conscientious objectors – known as 'conchies' – who became volunteer firemen. Conchies were pacifists who for various reasons refused to serve in the armed forces and harm other human beings. In the First World War they were regarded as traitors or lunatics and were sent to prison or to serve in the trenches as stretcher-bearers and ambulance drivers. In 1939, anyone who decided to be a conchie had to stand in front of a tribunal and argue their case. They were treated with more understanding and tolerance than in the previous war, but they could still end up behind bars. Their chances of avoiding a prison term improved dramatically if they offered to work in the fire service. As a result, a small tribe of artists, writers, sculptors and other peace-loving bohemians ended up risking their lives as Blitz firemen.

Burrow ignored the taunts and mocking insults directed against his colleagues. He knew that when the bombs started falling the criticism would stop.

In September 1940, there were 300 auxiliary fire stations scattered across Greater London and Henry Burrow had been posted to station 20U. His first taste of action was on September 5, two days before the infamous 'Black Saturday' raid, the attack that marked the beginning of the Blitz on the capital. Burrow and his team had been called to a fire at an oil depot on the eastern fringes of London. The men could see the smoke rising from miles away, but before they reached the entrance to the depot one of them spotted a German fighter diving towards them.

"Everybody out and find some cover," cried the driver.

The auxiliaries didn't need any encouragement. They were out of the taxi in a second, looking for a place to hide. Burrow crawled under a large steel truck that was parked at the side of the road. The next instant, bullets were ripping into the tarmac as the fighter machine-gunned them from the air. The

German raider soon flew off to look for more promising targets, leaving Burrow and his mates to dust themselves down and take a look around. They were rather shocked to discover that their hiding place was in fact a large fuel tanker.

Burrow served bravely through the long, unbroken series of raids after Black Saturday. He had earned the right to call himself a veteran fire fighter, and was a tried and trusted man on the team when he arrived for duty on December 29.

On the morning after the fire around St. Paul's, Burrow's wife went along to his station to help cook breakfast for the exhausted fire teams. When she got there, she met a group of women waiting at the entrance. None of their men had returned from the city raid and there was no news of what had happened to them. All they knew was that it had been a bad one. Whole blocks of buildings had been lost, and some streets were literally wiped off the map. Paternoster Row, in the heart of London's publishing trade, was razed to the ground and five million books were destroyed overnight. Eight churches were in ruins and St. Paul's Cathedral had only narrowly escaped disaster.

The following day, news came to the station that another member of Burrow's team was safe in a City hospital. This man gave Burrow's wife every detail of their ordeal. Skipper had tried his best to keep the others going, the man told her from his hospital bed, pleading with them not to give up hope in the burning street. Despite the severe pain in his hands, Burrow had driven them on until each man had fallen or vanished in the smoke. The hospital survivor had staggered off alone and somehow found a way out of the firestorm. But he thought it was unlikely that any of the others could have escaped.

The next evening, Mrs. Burrow and her son were at home when a policeman called. Skipper had been officially posted as missing, almost two days after the rescue squads had finished combing the area for survivors. Nobody was sure his body would ever be recovered, such was the intensity of the blaze.

On the following morning there was an urgent message from St. Bartholomew's Hospital in central London. They had a patient in their burns ward who answered Burrow's description. Mrs. Burrow raced to the hospital and found her husband alive and well, although rather dazed. His only serious injuries were to his hands. He described his rescue by a group of soldiers, who had found him wandering about in the ashes of the fire, hours after the end of the raid. Burrow wasn't sure how he'd ended up there. The last thing he remembered was stepping down to the cellar and drifting off to sleep. Then he described the apparition of their son and how it had saved his life.

Burrow had earned his living with his hands, so it was a huge blow when surgeons told him that he would never recover his manual dexterity. He'd lost so much muscle and tissue from his fingers, they doubted if he'd even be able to pick up light objects, or grip the steering wheel of a car. But Henry Burrow was in the habit of surprising people with his tenacity. After leaving the burns ward he was offered a job in one of the fire service's engine shops. Over the following months he gradually exercised his hands back to health, keeping them supple by applying special creams and lotions.

When his son was a bit older, Burrow took him for a stroll among the streets that twist around St. Paul's Cathedral. He wanted to return to the place where he'd almost died – and explain to the boy how he'd appeared in a vision among the flames that had saved his father's life.

THINGS THAT GO BUMP
IN THE NIGHT

The German pilot Karl Brüning glanced up at the sky and noticed a full moon hanging over the airbase. In its silvery light he could clearly see the rows of Heinkel bombers arranged across the landing strip. A few months earlier he would have been pleased to see the moon sparkling above as he set out on a mission. It always made it easier for his navigator to guide the bomber across the Channel and identify targets on the ground. But tonight, the bright moon struck Brüning as a deadly enemy. Something was hunting the Luftwaffe's bombers through the night skies, shadowing them and destroying them in sudden bursts of gunfire.

The losses had been quite small so far. Only around 20 crews had failed to return in the last two weeks. This was a tiny proportion of the massive German air fleet, but it was making the pilots jumpy. There were whispers that the RAF had discovered how to track the German air force's navigational radio beams. Perhaps they had developed a secret weapon, something that literally enabled them to see in the dark? Luftwaffe pilots had come up against 'night fighters' before, usually on patrol over Britain's burning cities. They knew that some of these planes had spotted them in the powerful searchlights sent up from the ground, but it was easy for the German bombers to take evasive action and slip away into darkness. In the opening months of the Blitz, RAF night fighters had little chance of intercepting a lone Heinkel in the vast, empty skies over Britain. But something new was guiding them to their prey, bringing them close enough to take careful aim with their cannons and machine guns. In full moonlight, Brüning worried that his bomber would stand out for miles.

In February 1941, atrocious weather conditions across the English Channel had grounded most German bombing operations. For a few precious weeks, there was a lull in the Blitz. Britain's battered cities and towns used this opportunity to repair and rebuild their damaged buildings. For most of the previous five months, German bombers had been pounding the country with high explosives. In January, despite two weeks of poor weather, they had carried out heavy raids against London and a range of new targets, including the vital ports of Bristol, Portsmouth and Cardiff. The German intruders seemed to be growing bolder, and RAF officials came under intense pressure to improve their record of knocking them out of the sky.

The whole business of the night raids was a source of extreme frustration for the RAF. Air force commanders had always admitted privately that the army's ack-ack barrage around Britain's cities was ineffective. The roar of the guns might have worked wonders for civilian morale. But, in the days before radar tracking, there was little chance of any shells hitting their targets. In 1940, it was estimated that it took up to 20,000 rounds of ammunition to bring down a single German plane.

Developments with radar positioning at the beginning of the war had allowed gunners to plot the speed and direction of approaching planes. (Previously, artillerymen had used huge earhorns pointed up at the sky, to listen out for the rumble of enemy engines.) But it was still very difficult to establish the exact altitude of a plane, and most shells exploded a long way from their targets. Gunners had other tools to help them, including searchlights. They were guided by a man with a pair of binoculars scanning the skies. Later in the war, the lights were controlled by more sophisticated methods, including radar. Barrage balloons were used as static weapons, to deter any low level attackers.

Other than ack-ack, the only way to defend a city against a hoard of enemy bombers was to send up patrols of fighters, or to use diversionary tricks. The RAF tried both, but each had serious drawbacks.

British fighter planes flew thousands of patrols during the air raids of 1940, often at considerable risk to their pilots. Hurricanes and Spitfires cruised at low speed, hoping to see the glimmer of a bomber in a searchlight. If they were lucky, the German plane would be trapped in the beam of light long enough for them to close in and attack. But this was rare. Inside the narrow fuselage of a Heinkel or Dornier, the 800-million-candlepower dazzle of a searchlight was enough to startle any pilot into immediate action. The Luftwaffe planes were quite agile compared to British bombers and they could easily shake off the beam.

When RAF fighter pilots rushed into the weave of searchlights and shell explosions around their targets, they suddenly got a taste of what it was like to fly through ack-ack. The difficulty of identifying planes correctly led to hundreds of friendly fire incidents in the Second World War, when gunners shot down planes from their own side. The RAF experimented with so-called 'fighter nights' to try to minimize this danger. They persuaded searchlight teams and gunners to give their pilots three-minute windows of peace and quiet when they could search for raiders. At a prearranged time, the defenders on the ground would stop firing and the night fighters would rush in, looking for a target in the darkness. But very few of the fighter night trials resulted in a single enemy kill.

The RAF had more success with beam-bending and other diversions. Their scientists could mimic the frequency and sound of the Luftwaffe's radio signals (used to guide planes to their target) and trick the German pilots into flying away from cities and over open country. They even went so far as to start huge fires burning, in the hope of persuading the Germans that they were over a blazing city and it was time to drop their bombs. It worked. Acres of open farmland and heath were bombed to bits by the confused air crews. Beam-bending managed to throw off some inexperienced pilots, but most crews were on the lookout for anyone tampering with their beams.

As the Blitz intensified, RAF scientists worked feverishly to develop a mobile radar system that could track bombers anywhere in the country. They had already constructed a network of radar stations along the south coast that had helped to win the Battle of Britain. But there was little radar cover inland which might enable British fighters to be guided to intercept German planes.

By March 1941, the RAF had six inland radar units, known as Ground Controlled Interception stations (or GCI) up and running. Each one had a staff of 80 technicians and plotters who could direct a radio-equipped night fighter to within a mile of a bomber target. From there, the pilot had a good chance of sighting the enemy plane, before closing in and attacking. This was a first step towards developing genuine Airborne Interception (AI) equipment for night fighters. British engineers were getting closer to giving their pilots eyes in the dark.

Karl Brüning hadn't flown a mission for almost three months when he climbed into the cockpit of his Heinkel He-111 on March 12, 1941. He'd been on leave over Christmas and his airfield in Chartres, France, was so rain-soaked that the grass landing strip was unusable.

Finally, on March 11, Brüning's commanders ordered him to a nearby airfield at Avord, which had a tarmac runway. Brüning and a three-man crew were ready at 21:00, with a full load of bombs destined for Birkenhead in the northwest of England.

The moon was brighter than ever as he crossed the English Channel. To his surprise, Brüning didn't meet any searchlights or ack-ack ranging around his plane. The lack of enemy activity made him nervous and he ordered his men to keep their eyes peeled for any British night fighters who might be up on patrol. His Heinkel was equipped with three MG 15 machine gun ports: in the nose, in the belly and on the roof (known as the *dorsal*). Some German bombers even had a rear machine gun, protruding from just under the plane's rudder. Brüning's crew primed the guns and peered out through toughened glass panels at the ghostly night skies. Visibility was close to perfect, and the men reasoned they should have a good chance of spotting any prowling Hurricanes.

But the next second, bullets ripped through the glass nose of the cockpit, tore through the fuselage and stopped both engines dead. Splattered with engine oil, sparks and fuel, the plane immediately burst into flames. Brüning could feel the blood streaming over his hands as he struggled to control the joystick. Through his headset, he could hear the radioman and mechanic screaming for help. They were lying injured in the rear of the plane.

With wounds in his left hand and foot, and the plane rapidly losing height in a dive, Brüning tried to take charge of the situation. He sent his navigator, Alexander Düssel, to tend to the wounded men and get their parachutes ready. In the meantime, he managed to level the plane, making it safer for his crew to jump. There was no chance of making a controlled landing, but perhaps they could still survive the attack? But then Düssel returned with disastrous news. The galley inside the plane was roaring with flames and impassable. He couldn't get through to the wounded men.

All Brüning could do was give the order to jump and hope that the two men in the rear of the plane would hear him and drag themselves to an escape hatch. As soon as he gave the command, Düssel drew back a glass panel in the side of the cockpit and threw himself out. He hadn't been wearing a parachute. Brüning stared out in shock at the black sky rushing past. He could only think that Düssel had lost his mind – or perhaps he couldn't find his parachute and was terrified of being consumed by the flames if he stayed inside the plane.

Brüning forced himself to set the autopilot and carefully checked his parachute for shrapnel rips or bullet holes. There was an escape hatch over his head and he slid the panel back while he was still sitting in his seat. It was only when he felt the thundering slipstream over the roof that he realized he might be tossed back onto the plane's burning rear-section if he jumped out from here. He slid out of his seat, making for the side hatch. It was then that he glanced through the glass nose of the cockpit and saw something lurking in the night, only yards away. It was a British *Boulton Paul Defiant* fighter, coming around for another shot. Brüning knew he had to get out before the Defiant's machine guns opened up. So he tumbled through the hatch, spinning away from his doomed plane as it streaked towards the ground.

A Boulton Paul Defiant night fighter

In the 1940s, radio sets and radar detectors were heavy, bulky items, which needed a two-man crew to work them properly. So the RAF decided to use their slower, workhorse fighter planes to carry AI instead of the smaller, faster Hurricanes and Spitfires. Their first attempt at installing AI was in a *Bristol Beaufighter*. It was a disappointing compromise. The only way to cram in all the radio equipment was to take all the guns out. So, to make up for the fighter's missing firepower, two Hurricane escorts had to accompany it. The radar detection worked reasonably well but, as soon as the Beaufighter dropped away, the Hurricane pilots only had seconds to close in for the kill. It was all too easy for them to lose sight of the target in the excitement of the attack.

Within a few months, scientists were developing versions of the AI boxes that were smaller and lighter. The RAF began fitting them into armed fighters, including Boulton Paul Defiants. This powerful fighter had a crew of two and was equipped with a dorsal four-gun turret. It had been withdrawn from service in the Battle of Britain, after suffering heavy losses in dogfights with the nimble Messerschmitt 109. But the plane's solid design made it an ideal night fighter. While the pilot acted as navigator and radar operator, keeping the Defiant on a steady course to the target, the gunner could take careful aim at the bomber's weakspots. The fighters were painted black and fitted with special exhausts that stopped any small flames from the engine giving away their position in the night sky.

Some Defiant pilots notched up several kills. Flying Officer Frederick Hughes and his gunner were night fighter aces, destroying 18 Luftwaffe planes. Karl Brüning's Heinkel bomber was one of them.

Brüning saw his bomber crash and explode below him, as he dangled from under his parachute. He landed in some shrubbery and began shouting for help. Although his wounds weren't painful, he knew there was no possibility of escaping back to Germany and he wanted to be treated as quickly as possible.

Two figures in the dark responded to his cries. As they approached him, Brüning heard them calling: "Hands up!"

It was a man and woman, some evacuees who were staying at the farm where Brüning had landed. They stared at him, clearly terrified. Brüning handed them his pistol and they relaxed slightly. The woman bandaged his hand and the man offered him a cigarette. Then they helped him to a Home Guard post, where he was handed a cup of tea and more cigarettes. Brüning was lucky. Germans who bailed out of their planes over British cities often met with a hostile reception. It was said that some of the crew from a German plane shot down over Buckingham Palace had been beaten to death by a furious mob.

When he'd finished his tea, Brüning was helped into an army truck and driven to a military base for questioning. His foot was bleeding and he was in some pain. But his interrogators stripped him naked and questioned him aggressively until dawn. At one point, they held a cigarette case up to his face: it had belonged to Düssel, whose body had been found in a field.

A few hours later, Brüning was taken to a hospital where surgeons operated on his foot. From there, he was dragged around a succession of army bases and interrogation rooms. Finally, he arrived at a German POW camp in Bury, in northern England, where he remained in detention for six and a half years.

On his repatriation to Germany in July 1947, Brüning joined the German domestic air services and went back to flying. Finally, in 1978, the Heinkel crash site was excavated and the last two members of Brüning's unfortunate crew were moved to a military cemetery in Staffordshire.

DOODLEBUGS AND ROCKETS

This drawing shows how tall the German Vengeance weapons were, compared to an ordinary house.

Wing Commander Donald Beaumont was on patrol with his squadron over England's south coast when his cockpit radio crackled into life: "Radar's picked up a diver. Get ready to intercept." Beaumont ordered his flight sergeant to accompany him and the two pilots turned their Hawker Tempest fighters out to sea. Beaumont scanned the horizon, searching for a tiny dot of orange flame rushing out of the dawn skies.

It was June 16, 1944 and the Germans had just unleashed a strange, new weapon in their Blitz on Britain: the flying bomb, nicknamed the 'diver' by the RAF, after a character in a radio comedy show. Only half the size of a regular fighter plane and powered by crude jet engines, these pilotless missiles carried 850 kilos (1,900lbs) of explosive. Set to explode on impact with the ground, divers were causing mayhem in the heart of London.

Beaumont didn't know if he could stop the mysterious German weapon that was thundering towards him. Radar trackers estimated that the bombs flew on a steady course at low altitude and reached incredible speeds - up to 720kmh (450mph) or more. The army's gun emplacements couldn't target anything moving at this pace, and regular Spitfires and Hurricanes were too slow to intercept them. But Beaumont's Tempest had a maximum speed of around 690kmh (430mph). It was just possible he might be able to catch and somehow destroy it.

Even with over 400 hours of flying time and plenty of combat experience under his belt, Beaumont's heart was pounding. He was used to going into a dogfight against another flesh and blood pilot - not pitting his wits against a machine. And how could he get close enough to the bomb to blow it up, without being caught in the explosion? The next instant these questions disappeared from his mind as he spotted a black smudge racing towards him. It was topped with a brilliant point of light – a jet burner.

Beaumont immediately yanked the joystick to one side, almost losing consciousness as he wheeled his Tempest in a dizzying turn. By the time he'd completed the turn, the flying bomb had already passed him and was vanishing into the clouds. The two RAF pilots followed in pursuit. But, even at full throttle, they couldn't close the gap with the jet-propelled missile.

With only moments remaining before the bomb crashed into London, Beaumont tried to hit it with a long blast from his fighter's four cannons. He was too far off to destroy the bomb, but he managed to damage one of its wings and slow it down. When he tried firing again, Beaumont cursed – his guns were empty. But his flight sergeant saved the day, flashing over Beaumont's wingtip and firing a long blast at the ailing flying bomb. The sinister tube rolled over and dived into a field, sending up a great cloud of smoke and flames as it exploded.

Although the Luftwaffe remained a powerful force until the last year of the Second World War, by the summer of 1942 the Allies were mounting huge bombing raids on German cities from airfields across England. After a massive firebomb attack on the historic port of Lübeck, an enraged Hitler ordered revenge attacks against British civilian targets. The Luftwaffe responded by attacking some of Britain's prettiest cities, in what became known as the Baedeker Raids. The story goes that they chose their targets from a popular travel guidebook of the same name. But they also pumped money into secret weapons research. The result was a series of fantastic inventions: the *Vergeltungswaffe*, or Vengeance weapons.

In early 1943, British Intelligence officers heard some startling whispers about a secret research station located in Peenemünde, an isolated island in the Baltic, off the north German coast. Locals reported explosions and flashes in the night sky and odd-looking machines being built on concrete platforms.

The RAF sent reconnaissance pilots on a mission and were shocked by the photographs they brought back. Even from very high altitude, it was possible to see clearly dozens of rockets under construction, each standing around 12m (40 feet) high. There were other peculiar objects scattered around the site, but nobody could identify them. It was a junior Women's Auxiliary Air Force officer who guessed what they might be: ramps. Each ramp had another object resting upon it, which she thought might be small planes. From the blackened tarmac around the base of the ramps, scientists deduced that the planes must be fitted with fuel-burning engines, rather than propellers. That would make them incredibly fast, and might even give them the range to reach London.

The RAF's Bomber Command didn't delay. British aircrews pounded the rocket site with high explosives. Although it was a huge blow to the Luftwaffe's plans, the raid wasn't a complete success. German technicians moved their surviving equipment to underground bunkers and secret airfields in France and Holland and were soon assembling a fleet of their deadly jet weapons. A week after the D-Day landings in Normandy, they were finally ready to send rockets screaming across the English Channel.

German scientists and engineers were world leaders when it came to armaments design and Hitler had always supported their projects – no matter how far-fetched they seemed. With his troops vastly outnumbered and busy fighting a global war, he dreamed of a missile that could leap continents and oceans. His scientists tried to satisfy this craving for a long-range weapon by experimenting with jet engines and rockets. Their first successful device was the Vengeance weapon No.1 – or the V-1.

Like many brilliant inventions, its design was quite simple. It was essentially a small, steel plane packed with explosives, that was pushed through the air by the thrust of a jet engine's exhaust gasses. Aviation designers had been experimenting with jet engines long before the war started, but the Germans were the first to manufacture them in great numbers. They bolted the engine to the roof of the V-1 and fired it from a ramp. It had enough fuel to fly for 30 minutes, giving it a range of around 480km (300 miles).

The guidance system was ingenious, to say the least. A set of instrument boxes, compasses, pendulums and spinning gyroscopes maintained the jet's balance, height and course. To send it down to earth, the bomb relied on a small propeller hidden in its nose. German technicians at the launch site tried to estimate how many times this propeller should turn on the flight to London. They could then preset the propeller to switch the bomb's height controls to zero feet when it was over the target, sending the machine into a vertical dive.

As it fell to ground, the bomb's fuel pipes ran dry and its engine suddenly cut out. For several seconds, the V-1 rushed through the air in silence, followed by a huge explosion. This loss of power during the dive was a German design fault. But the terrifying suspense of these last, silent seconds earned the weapon a dreaded reputation.

Missiles are complicated beasts and even with its amazing design innovations the V-1 was notoriously inaccurate. To remedy this, the Germans briefly considered using pilots to steer them towards their targets. They called in one of their leading test pilots, Hanna Reitsch, to conduct a series of daring test flights to see if this was possible.

Reitsch was an aviation prodigy, famed for being the first woman to cross the Alps in a glider, as well as for dozens of other flying feats. She was a fervent Nazi, had been awarded the Iron Cross for bravery, and counted Hitler as a personal friend. Reitsch was also an experienced test pilot and had flown prototypes of the Luftwaffe's Stuka and Dornier warplanes. She was thrilled at the prospect of testing a flying bomb.

Reitsch's V-1 was fitted with wooden skids – she was hoping to land it – and dropped from the belly of a Heinkel bomber at high altitude. With the jet engine spluttering and booming directly above the canopy of her cockpit, Reitsch struggled to control the flying bomb. On a straight and level course it handled quite well. But the V-1 was a point and shoot weapon, and hadn't been designed for fancy acrobatics. Reitsch's landing was more like a controlled crash than a regular put down. But, thanks to her quick reflexes and natural talent, she got down safely.

Reitsch made several other disappointing test flights in V-1s, until the Luftwaffe finally scrapped the idea of using pilots to fly them. Instead, they concentrated their efforts on improving the jet's internal guidance instruments. Research scientists weren't expecting to achieve pinpoint accuracy, but if they could hit a large city there was a chance that the V-1 might change the course of the war.

In the early hours of June 13, 1944, the first flying bombs landed on London, heralding a new, terrifying chapter in the story of the Blitz. Their explosive force flattened houses, maimed and killed, but the weapon had other demoralizing effects on the capital's war-weary residents. When they heard the sputtering growl of a V-1's engine approaching, people immediately looked up at the sky. As if in some kind of trance, they followed what they nicknamed buzz bombs, or *doodlebugs*, on their course across the city skyline, with the awful knowledge that when the engine cut out the bomb would plunge to the ground. Diners in restaurants broke off their conversations as a V-1 passed overhead, ready to dive for cover if there was a sudden, eerie silence. The rasping, grating roar of the jet engine could be heard for miles.

In Greater London, where almost 2,500 V-1s exploded, this sound began to dominate everyday life. As with the first Luftwaffe attacks in the Blitz, the army and air force seemed powerless to stop it. Only weeks earlier, Londoners had been celebrating the Allied advances into Normandy. There was a new, confident mood returning to the capital after years of bloodshed and suffering. But, suddenly, the Germans were striking back harder than ever, and the invasion of France seemed all but forgotten.

From the middle of June 1944, V-1s were screaming across London at a rate of up to 100 attacks per day. They came in the daylight hours, when people were out and about, away from their shelters. Striking the city when it was teeming with life, a single bomb could result in a shocking number of casualties.

On the morning of June 18, the congregation of the Guards' Chapel near Buckingham Palace was in the middle of the Sunday service, when the cough and growl of an approaching V-1 interrupted the sermon. There were 180 people in the church, a mixed group of soldiers and civilians. They all must have known that as long as the jet engine kept rumbling, they would be safe. But, to their horror, silence settled around the church hall. Seconds later, the bomb crashed into the roof and exploded, killing 119 of the congregation instantly.

Rescue workers slaved for 48 hours to dig out the survivors. This was the worst V-1 outrage of the war, but the newspapers barely mentioned it. To prevent the Germans from charting the accuracy of their attacks, they were under strict government censorship.

Londoners felt their plight was being hidden from the rest of the country. As the weeks rolled by and the bombs kept coming, they wondered how long their city could hold out.

Wing Commander Beaumont didn't have long to wait for his next tussle with a doodlebug. Only two days after his first successful interception, he was making a solo patrol over the town of Hastings when he received a radio warning. There was a buzz bomb coming towards him, flying at an altitude 300m (1000 feet) below his Tempest. Beaumont quickly pushed his fighter into a dive, picking up as much speed as he could before meeting his target. It wasn't hard to spot the V-1, streaking over the Channel. Pilots could see the sinister orange glow of the rocket's exhaust from miles away. Beaumont carefully adjusted the cockpit controls, so he was on a collision course with the jet bomb and armed his guns. The 23-year-old Battle of Britain veteran was determined that, on this occasion, his guns alone would be enough to stop the V-1 intruder.

Beaumont's Tempest had reached a shuddering 720kmh (450mph) when the V-1 crossed over his gun sights. From only a few hundred yards away, Beaumont pumped the firing button and watched his cannon shells tearing into the missile's steel fuselage, punching holes through its wings. But the V-1 held its course. Now in a steep dive, Beaumont waited until the last possible second, then fired a single, long burst.

Suddenly, he was lost inside a huge fireball of black smoke, flames and twisted steel. The V-1 had exploded before he'd had a chance to veer away. Beaumont's Tempest was rocking and bucking in the heart of the blast. He was thrown violently into the side of the cabin and the plane went into a roll. When he finally shot through the smoke and into light, Beaumont saw his flight uniform was smoking. Flames had licked through into the cockpit and singed his clothes – but he was unhurt. The only damage to his plane was some burning and bubbling of the paint along the fuselage. He'd escaped destruction by a split second. Beaumont checked his course and turned for home, leaving behind him a cloud of shattered metal dropping quickly to earth.

After his successful attack, Beaumont realized the only effective way to tackle the German flying bombs was to combine early radar sightings with constant patrols by fighter interceptors, flying at high altitude so they could dive down on the raiders. In a special plan called *Operation Diver*, the RAF gave Beaumont and his squadron of Tempests total control of the airspace along the V-1 flight paths, nicknamed Doodlebug Alleys because of the large numbers of flying bombs that used them. Artillery fire was restricted and slower fighter planes were banned from the area. Several Tempests had already been mistaken for the V-1s they were chasing, and fired upon by their own side. Beaumont also asked for a screen of barrage balloons to be raised around London, floating at the same altitude as the V-1s. This was his only tactical mistake; the wing tips of the V-1s were fitted with razor-sharp cable cutters, designed to slice through balloon snares.

In June 1944, around half of the flying bombs detected by British radar pierced London's skies. But, by July, *Operation Diver* was up and running and only a third were making it through the net. The figures for August were even better: just 17% of the divers were reaching their target area. Thanks to a new invention – the proximity fuse – which used radio waves to detonate a shell when it was close to its target, British artillery teams began stopping more of the flying bombs. For Beaumont's pilots, the business of intercepting V-1s became a matter of routine.

Wing Commander Beaumont even discovered how to knock flying bombs out of the sky without firing his guns. He was flying over Hastings again, hunting for a V-1 in high cloud. Radio reports told him the bomb was closing on him, but he couldn't see the telltale glow of the jet exhaust. Then he spotted an opening in some clouds below. Beaumont pushed the joystick forward and put his Tempest into a steep dive. Perhaps he could find his way into clear sky and spot the raider?

The bomb wasn't hard to find. It came hurtling out of the gap in the clouds he was diving for. Beaumont had no time to arm his guns or veer away. With seconds to go before his plane and the V-1 collided, he decided his best chance of escape was to speed up and nip across the path of the raider. Pushing the throttle to maximum, Beaumont streaked ahead of the V-1 with only inches to spare. Pulling out of his dive he blew a sigh of relief, then banked and got ready for a chase. But the V-1 had vanished. Suddenly, at the edge of his vision, he saw a bright flash in the patchwork of fields below. It must have been the jet, falling out of control before exploding. Beaumont was puzzled for a moment. Then he realized that the turbulence of his own aircraft so close to the V-1 must have upset its delicate guidance mechanisms.

Later that day, he was out on another patrol when coastal radar stations picked up a cluster of incoming V-1s. Beaumont intercepted and destroyed one and took off in pursuit of another. Closing quickly, he armed the guns for an easy kill. But when he pressed the firing button, his guns clicked empty. With no other fighters nearby, Beaumont racked his mind for a way to stop the flying bomb. Flying alongside the weapon, he began edging his wingtip closer towards it. He considered flipping the V-1's wing, to send it tumbling to the ground. But he was an experienced pilot and he decided that making contact with another object at such high speed was too risky. Instead, he began to wonder if the turbulence from his wingtip might be enough to disturb the V-1, as it had done that morning?

At a speed of close to 640kmh (400mph) Beaumont dipped his wing and edged over to the raider. Gradually he began raising the wing, until it was only a few inches below the V-1's wingtip. After a few seconds, the disturbed air passing over Beaumont's wing began to destabilize the V-1's flight. The Wing Commander watched in amazement as the German bomb rolled away and tumbled to the ground.

With the threat of the V-1s receding, Londoners thought they were finally safe from the Luftwaffe's attacks. But, at dawn on September 8, the whole of west London was shaken by a massive explosion, followed by a sound like a thunderclap. Local officials said a gas main in the suburb of Chiswick had blown up, leaving nothing behind but a huge crater. But nobody believed it. The city was soon buzzing with whispers of German rockets and spaceships dropping out of the sky. By the following week, there were three or four unexplained blasts in the capital every day. But it wasn't until November 10, 1944, that Churchill announced the truth to the nation. London was coming under attack from a new vengeance weapon: the V-2.

German inventors had built a rocket bomb that was the first man-made object to enter space. Compared to the V-1, it was a complex machine, reaching an incredible speed of 4,800kmh (3,000mph). It moved so quickly, scraping the stratosphere in an arc 100km (60 miles) high, that survivors reported hearing the noise of its engine and a sonic boom well after the initial explosion. It came without warning. Anything within hundreds of yards of a landing rocket was obliterated by its huge explosive warhead.

For Londoners, the noise of a V-2 was like the crack of doom. Around 600 of the rockets hit the capital, killing and injuring at least 7,000 people. Nothing could stop them – except Allied bombing attacks against the trucks they were launched from, in German-occupied territory. The rockets were terrifying weapons, but they were also impractical. Each machine cost the same as a large bomber and needed precious, lightweight metals for its construction. Germany's war factories and production lines were almost in ruins when the V-2 was first launched against London. The Luftwaffe had been destroyed and on every front the Allies were crushing the German army. It was simply impossible to produce the rocket in large enough numbers to change the course of war.

London suffered another string of terrible incidents, including a hit on a department store just before Christmas, when 168 people died. But however horrific they were, the V-2 strikes remained isolated events. Meanwhile, the Allies were advancing steadily towards Berlin, and final victory over Hitler. The last Vengeance weapon to strike England was fired on March 28, 1945. German rocket bases were soon in the hands of the Allies. Vast amounts of research equipment, spare parts and scientists were shipped across the Atlantic. The Americans had good reason to celebrate the end of the rockets. In the closing days of the war, the Germans were perfecting a new, longer-range V-2, capable of reaching New York. The Vengeance weapons represented the last desperate strikes of the Nazi war machine. But despite their incredible, destructive power, they were too late to save Germany from defeat.

Wing Commander Beaumont went on to destroy 31 of the V-1 raiders. His Tempest was shot down over enemy territory in October 1944, but he survived the crash and spent the rest of the war in a POW camp. On his return to England Beaumont took up a career as a test pilot, and in 1948 he became the first Briton to fly faster than the speed of sound.

THE BLITZ SPIRIT

In the first week of the 1940 air raids, writers and journalists described the amazing courage shown by ordinary Londoners. There was, they claimed, no panic or misery in the public shelters. Instead, the locals refused to be ruffled by the German attacks. They drank tea and played cards as the walls shook around them. They offered complete strangers shelter in their homes and never grumbled about their hardships. These reports started people talking about some kind of Blitz spirit, a proud, determined attitude shared by rich and poor alike. But did the British really behave this way, or is it just a myth that has grown up since the end of the war? Nobody doubts that they suffered horrors in the air raids. But just how long and hard was the battle on the Home Front?

The Blitz itself began with the heavy raids on London on September 7, 1940, and lasted until May 16, 1941. But, for the Germans, the air campaign stretched across several years and thousands of missions. They didn't recognize a separate Battle of Britain, as the RAF did. Each side had different perceptions of what was happening in the air war – and who was winning it.

The Germans argued that they were still only targeting military areas, but this claim is hard to believe. Their bombers were dropping parachute mines, that could drift anywhere over a city, and pounding residential areas with high explosives. With the exception of November 2, when bad weather grounded their planes, the Luftwaffe bombed London for the following 76 nights, until more poor weather interrupted the raids again in early January 1941.

After a lull in the battle in February – thanks to thick snowstorms over the Channel – a second phase of the Blitz began in March 1941. This time, the Germans broadened their attack, bombing ports and industrial targets in the north of England, as well as Glasgow, Plymouth and Belfast.

After a particularly ferocious attack on London, on May 10, 1941, many people feared the Germans were softening up the capital, prior to launching a full-scale invasion. It's true Hitler had an invasion planned – but it had nothing to do with Britain. Flushed with the success of Blitzkrieg, he went on to launch *Operation Barbarossa* on June 22, declaring war on his unsuspecting ally, the Soviet Union. From that point on, the Luftwaffe armada flew east, abandoning their attempts to crush Britain's fighting spirit through aerial bombing.

Over the next two years, there were still occasional, light raids across England, but it wasn't until February 1944 that a new phase of the air war began. This

'Little Blitz' lasted until April 1944. After another lull, the peace was shattered by the arrival of the Vengeance weapons in June.

The British had endured a long and ruthless series of attacks and, on the face of it, they had managed to carry on with business as usual. There had been no major riots or civil disturbances. On the whole, people had kept their cool, tolerating the discomfort of their Anderson shelters and the irritations of rationing and the blackout. Everyone had tried to keep up with their work, turning up at offices and factories every morning, even when there was a good chance they'd arrive to find a pile of smoking rubble where their desk had once been.

Some people even looked for a funny side to the bombing. Businesses put chalkboard signs outside their shattered premises, reading:

More open than usual.

If you think this is bad, you should see our Berlin branch.

Outside a damaged barber's there was the sign:
We specialize in close shaves.

British newspapers liked to present the average Blitz survivor as a plucky Cockney, proud and defiant as the bombs came raining down. They used photographs of the crowds sheltering in the Underground to show the unity and common purpose of the nation. They talked of everyone being in it together, all facing an equal danger from the bombs.

Many people did show incredible resilience and bravery in the Blitz years, but it's not true that they all suddenly pulled together, or that they were all in the same danger. The rich, unsurprisingly, had a much easier time than most. Even when they didn't have a country house to retire to, wealthy Londoners could at least afford to construct comfortable shelters for themselves. In the early years of the war, they were still able to visit restaurants and splurge on lavish meals and wine. They had fuel for their cars and occasional luxuries like a new suit of clothes or a tin of black market jam. But most ordinary people didn't enjoy these distractions from the bombing. Their only concern was staying alive.

Perhaps the most amazing thing about the German air war against Britain was that it failed. Even after months of nightly raids, London was still a working city. The Luftwaffe's Heinkel and Dornier bombers just couldn't deliver the huge bomb loads needed to destroy it. In contrast, the American B17 *Flying Fortress* bomber could carry almost four times the same weight of explosives as a German raider. The Luftwaffe had other problems. Their fighter escorts ran out of fuel after 20 minutes of flying time over England, and they didn't have the right equipment for accurate bomb aiming.

Over 40,000 people lost their lives in air raids during the Blitz – and over 60,000 in the war as a whole. Although this is a terrible figure, it doesn't compare with the casualties in air raids by the Allies, later in the war. In Tokyo, Hamburg and Dresden, tens of thousands were killed in single attacks. But Britain's politicians and military experts had been so convinced their country was facing complete destruction in the run up to war, it's not surprising that they turned the whole Blitz experience into a glorious victory. Some air raid survivors had been heroes, and risked their lives to save others. But most people were just trying to look after themselves and their loved ones, in a vicious and pitiless war.

GLOSSARY

This glossary explains some of the technical, military and other words you will come across in the book. If a word in an entry is in *italic* type, it means it has an entry of its own.

ack-ack   Anti-aircraft *artillery* fire.
AI   Short for Airborne Interception, this was *radar* equipment used to guide fighter planes towards enemy bombers at night.
air raid   An attack by *bomber* planes.
Allies   The countries fighting Germany and its Allies (known as the *Axis* powers) in the Second World War. Britain, the Soviet Union and the USA were the main Allied nations.
Anderson shelter   A small, steel *air raid* shelter, installed in private gardens.
armada   A large fleet of ships or planes.
armaments   An army's weapons and *munitions*.
ARP   Stands for Air Raid Precautions, the emergency services dealing with *air raids*.
artillery   Large, mobile guns firing *shells*.
Axis powers   The countries fighting the *Allies* during the Second World War. The main members of the Axis were Germany, Italy and Japan.
barrage   Steady *artillery* fire against *infantry*, ships or aircraft.

GLOSSARY

barrage balloons   Large, floating balloons, also known as blimps, that prevented planes from flying at a low height.

Battle of Britain   The intense air battle between German and British planes over the English Channel and southern England, which began on July 10, 1940 and ended with the beginning of the *Blitz*.

battleship   A large, heavily armed warship.

biplane   A plane with two sets of wings, one above the other.

blackout   Hiding all sources of light to make it difficult for enemy planes to navigate.

Black Saturday   A heavy *air raid* that took place in London on September 7, 1940, which marked the beginning of the *Blitz*.

Blitz   The period of heavy bombing by German planes on London and other British cities from September 7, 1940 to May 16, 1941

Blitzkrieg   A military attack which relies on firepower, speed and surprise. This often refers to the rapid German invasion of Denmark, Norway, Belgium, Holland, Luxembourg and France in the early part of the Second World War

Bofor   An *ack-ack* gun that could be mounted on a truck.

bomb cemetery   An area of open ground used to dismantle and explode *UXBs*.

bomber   A plane with a cargo of bombs.

bomber's moon   A full or bright moon that helped German air crews to navigate.

cannon A gun mounted in a fighter plane that fires small *shells*.

civilian Anyone or anything not part of the armed forces.

conchie Short for conscientious objector, someone who refuses to fight in a war because of their beliefs.

diver An RAF term for the *V-1*.

dogfight A duel between two fighter planes.

doodlebug A popular term for a *V-1* flying bomb.

Dornier A German bomber plane used in the *Blitz*.

dorsal A machine gun port on the roof of a plane.

emplacement A fortified position for troops or guns.

evacuation The mass-movement of *civilians* away from dangerous areas during wartime.

firewatcher A lookout on a building, guarding against *incendiary bombs*.

friendly fire The accidental shooting down of a vehicle or soldier by their own side.

fuselage The main part of a plane that holds the crew or cargo.

gunner Another name for an artilleryman, a soldier (or sailor) who specializes in guns.

Heavy Rescue Branch of the *ARP* who saved people from collapsed buildings.

Heinkel He-111 A German bomber plane used extensively against Britain during the *Blitz*.

Home Front Anyone or anything in the home country during a foreign war.

incendiary A bomb, or fuel, designed to start fires.

incident The damage caused by an exploding bomb.

infantry Soldiers who fight mostly on foot.

Kriegsmarine The German navy.

land girls Female volunteers who worked on British farms during the Second World War.

Little Blitz The renewed period of German air attacks between February and April 1944.

Luftwaffe The German air force.

mine An explosive device hidden underwater or below ground.

Morrison shelter A small, steel *air-raid* shelter, for use indoors.

munitions Ammunition, including bullets and *shells*.

Nazi A member of Hitler's political party.

night fighter A fighter plane adapted for use at night.

occupied territory Land under the control of an enemy power.

panzer A German steel-plated tank or vehicle.

paratrooper A soldier who goes into battle jumping from a plane, using a parachute.

pea-souper A thick fog caused by air pollution and cold weather.

phoney war The name given to the quiet period between September 1939 to April 1940 when there was little fighting in Europe.

radar Short for Radio Detection and Ranging, a method of fixing the position of an object using radio waves.

RAF Short for Royal Air Force.

rationing Strict control of how much food and other goods someone is allowed.

GLOSSARY

reconnaissance The inspection of an area, to gather information in advance of a military operation.

salvo Several large guns firing at the same instant.

sapper An army engineer, skilled in defusing and clearing *mines*.

scramble Pilot slang for getting planes off the ground.

shells A missile fired from *artillery* or *cannons*, packed with explosive.

solo When a pilot flies alone.

Spitfire A British fighter plane, much admired for its agility and advanced design.

squadron A small unit of cavalry, aircraft or naval vessels.

stormtrooper A German soldier specializing in sudden, *blitzkrieg* attacks.

strafe To machine gun from the air.

Stuka A German dive bomber attack plane.

surface shelter A brick *air raid* shelter open to the public.

UXB The abbreviation for an unexploded bomb.

Vengeance weapons German weapons which included the *V-1* and *V-2*.

V-1 A German jet-propelled flying bomb, also known as a *doodlebug*.

V-2 A German rocket bomb.

X-Gerät A radio beam that helped German pilots to navigate to their targets.

Zeppelin A large German airship used in the First World War.

USBORNE QUICKLINKS

For links to exciting websites where you can listen to air-raid sirens, build your own shelter, watch a movie clip of V rockets in action, read original documents from the War Cabinet in London and find out more about the Second World War, go to the Usborne Quicklinks Website at www.usborne-quicklinks.com and enter the keywords "true stories blitz".

INTERNET SAFETY

When using the Internet, make sure you follow these safety guidelines:

- Ask an adult's permission before using the Internet.

- Never give out personal information, such as your name, address or telephone number.

- If a website asks you to type in your name or email address, check with an adult first.

- If you receive an email from someone you don't know, don't reply to it.

TRUE STORIES OF THE SECOND WORLD WAR

Paul Dowswell

This time two torpedoes hit home. One caused only minor damage. The other went off underneath the stern, with a huge watery explosion that shot like a whiplash through the length of the ship. It buckled deck plates and bulkheads, and threw men to the floor or against metal partitions and instruments, with breathtaking violence. Above the site of the explosion, water surged into the ship with a vengeance, flooding the entire steering compartment.

Epic encounters between titanic warships, battles involving thousands of men, and duels between lone snipers facing almost certain death are just some of the dramatic tales in this gripping collection of stories from the Second World War.

Also from Usborne True Stories

TRUE STORIES OF HEROES

Paul Dowswell

His blood ran cold and Perevozchenko was seized by panic. He knew that his body was absorbing lethal doses of radiation, but instead of fleeing he stayed to search for his colleague. Peering into the dark through a broken window, he could see only a mass of tangled wreckage. By now he had absorbed so much radiation he felt his whole body was on fire. But then he remembered that there were several other men near to the explosion who might be trapped...

From firefighters battling with a blazing nuclear reactor to a helicopter rescue team on board a fast-sinking ship, this is an amazingly vivid collection of stories about men and women whose extraordinary courage has captured the imagination of millions.

Shortlisted for the Blue Peter Book Awards 2002

TRUE
ESCAPE
STORIES

Paul Dowswell

Finally, the night had come to take a trip to the roof. Morris spent the day beforehand trying to curb his restlessness. What if the way up to the roof was blocked? What if the ventilator motor had been replaced after all? All their painstaking work would be wasted. The 12-year sentence stretched out before him. Then another awful thought occurred. The holes in the wall would be discovered eventually, and that would mean even more years added on to his sentence.

As well as locked doors, high walls and barbed wire, many escaping prisoners also face savage dogs and armed guards who shoot to kill. From Alcatraz to Devil's Island, read the extraordinary tales of people who risked their lives for their freedom.

Also from Usborne True Stories

TRUE
SPY
STORIES

Paul Dowswell & Fergus Fleming

"In all your years of fame," Kramer explained delicately, "you have known some of the most powerful men in Europe. Would you consider returning to Paris now to mingle again with these influential gentlemen? And, while you're doing this, might you be able to keep me informed of anything interesting they might say?"

Margaretha looked curious but non-committal.

Kramer went on, "We could pay you well for this information — say 24,000 francs."

What are real spies like? Some, like beautiful Mata Hari, are every bit as glamorous as famous fictional agents such as James Bond. But spies usually live shadowy double lives, risking prison, torture and execution for a chance to change history.